HAPPY
Beginnings

HOW I BECAME
MY OWN
*F*AIRY *G*ODMOTHER!

By
*L*ORENA *B*ATHEY

Published by
Scepter Press
www.scepter-press.com
info@scepter-press.com
877-782-6464

Edited by
Awareness Publishing Company LLC
5224 N. Summit Street
Toledo, Ohio, 43611   USA

Designed by
Roy Rezentes II

This book is printed on acid-free paper.

ISBN 0-9776811-0-6
Library of Congress Number 2005911069

Dedication

To all the women that found
the endings in their life allowed their
"Happy Beginnings" to emerge.

Acknowledgments

To my friends: Nancy, Susan, Stephanie, Rebecca, Rachel, Lisa, Erin, Diana, and Joanna. Thank you for your unwavering support in my talents and ideas. Without you all, I could never have accomplished my dream!

To my children, who inspire me every day to be a better person.

To my family, for always being a sustaining force in my life.

To S, thank you for your belief in my ability and loving me exactly as I am.

To Donna, for pitching, pushing, and making sure my story was heard.

To Sandy, for making my writing coherent.

To Roy, for saving the day and making my vision a reality.

To the Source, thank for always showing me at exactly the right moment that I was able to be everything I should be. Thank you for putting all the right people and moments in place to allow me to make my dreams my reality.

Foreword

It took two years for this story to unfold. My reason for sharing my experiences is that I have found in speaking with many divorced women that many of the ways that I experienced events, they too went through. My purpose in sharing all the details of my life is to let other women know they are not alone and to hopefully give a woman the heart to make her circumstances in life better by extracting herself from a bad situation. However, the message of this book is to give you encouragement to release the "*real you*" that has been locked away in the closet or attic of your mind. That "*real you*" is always waiting for your strength to begin living the life you were meant to live. It takes great courage and bravery to make that step, and I know that you have all that within you.

I hope this book makes you laugh, cry and *feel* in great depth. I welcome any questions or comments that you might have after reading *Happy Beginnings*. I hope that in some way I can help you realize that sometimes through the greatest of pains can come the freedom to become your own fairy godmother and wave your wand to make your dreams come true.

CHAPTER ONE

It's begun

As I sat watching my favorite television series, I was appalled that the main character's boyfriend had just broken up with her on a post-it note. I was completely unaware that a similar fate awaited me but on a slightly larger stationery product.

My husband sat across from me with his 3x5 index card neatly printed with bullet points outlining why he was moving out of our home.

Bullet Point No 1: "I'm not happy."

Bullet Point No 2: "I need some space."

Bullet Point No. 3: "I'm not sure I am still in love with you." And just like that, I was going to be alone. The reason was not that my husband died in a plane crash, as I had always feared. It was not because he had a stress heart attack in a hotel room while on a business trip. The reason was staring at me holding a 3x5-index card and telling me that he was not sure that he was still "in" love with me. I heard the words coming at me at supersonic speed. I heard the words in slow motion. I heard the words…wait…I did not hear the words. "What?" I asked, "What did you say?"

"I think that we need to take a break. I need time to find out some things. I have rented an apartment," he told me again.
"A what?" I asked.
My husband looked at me funny. "I rented a furnished apartment."
"Where?" I inquired.
"Near to my work," he answered.

The words sunk below my subcutaneous layer. The neurons began to fire in my brain; and I felt a rush of anger, hurt, betrayal, astonishment, and incredulousness come surging up from my soul and out of my mouth.
"We just got back from vacation. What do you mean you are moving out? What is going on? Are you having an affair? When did you decide to do this? Oh, my God, I am going to be a statistic."

I could no longer sit, so I got up from the couch and paced. Then my heart absorbed the emotions, and I had to sit down before I fell down.
"Get out now." I said with eerie calm.
My husband looked scared.
"I can't." he looked at me sheepishly.
"What do you mean? You have an apartment, so go there."
My heart was icing over slowly.
"It won't be ready until Wednesday." He could not look at me while he said this.
"Are you kidding me? You just tell me that you are leaving me, but you're not leaving for three days?" I laughed in spite of myself. "I don't care where you go but you will not be here tonight. I do not want to see you, touch you, smell you, or even sense your presence. You are…"

I stopped and picked up the pillow off the couch. I looked at it and I felt the tingling in my hand as I lobbed it at him. I threw another, and another, and another. I was throwing the pillows at him as hard as I could. It was a one-sided pillow fight. My husband stared up at me, and I saw the anger come to his eyes. I thought how ludicrous it was that he was angry. He stood up and started to walk away.

"I am not leaving until Wednesday and you are going to have to find a way to deal with that." He was taking a big risk thinking that he was going to sleep peacefully next to me, after what he had just told me.

"No. You want to leave. You leave now!" I was adamant and this time, he looked downright scared.

"What about the kids?" he questioned.

"Now you're worried about the kids?" I wanted to smack him but I was out of pillows.

"I love the kids and I don't want to hurt them." He lowered his head when he realized how futile the sentence sounded.

"Really? Well, I think that their father leaving their mother the day after they come back from their summer vacation will be a very happy occasion for them, don't you?"

I knew I was being petty and hurtful, but I did not care. I did not want to look at this man any longer. Yet he was still there. His apartment was not going to be ready for three more days, and amazingly, he thought that staying at the house until the apartment became available was a viable option. I had met my husband when I was twenty-seven. We worked together in the same office and I was attracted to his quiet stability. We had very dissimilar personalities but I loved him and believed that we could have a happy life together. I was loud and emotional while he was quiet and consistent. With the naiveté of age, I believed that we could overcome any obstacles. I was a good wife. I varied menus for dinner, kept the house clean, and I tried to be a good support for my husband.

Yet, as the years went on and we added two children to our family, my dissatisfaction grew. It seemed as the pressures of life continued, my husband and I began walking two different paths. His path was to work, work, and then work some more. Mine was to be the epitome of mother and wifehood. Our differences in personality grew and the environment of graduating resentment took hold.

After I recognized that our relationship was terminal, I stayed in the marriage even with my unhappiness, because I felt there was nowhere else to go. I was a stay-at-home mom that had been out of the workforce for many years and had no true belief that I could make it on my own. My husband fostered this by controlling all the money and most of the decision-making in our household. With this suppression our intimacy waned and while we were the picture of the happy family on the outside, behind the front door was a flat and tired relationship.

The catalyst to monumental changes in my life occurred when my mother passed away from cancer. I realized part of my decision for allowing my unhappiness was to make sure I pleased her, my family, and my husband. After her death and the subsequent expedited remarriage of my father, I found myself faltering in who I was. While my marriage had been for many years less than satisfying, I felt that this was my lot and accepted my life as it was. With my mother gone and the pressure of having to be perceived in a certain way lessened, I attempted to talk to my husband and tell him that things were not working well for us. He maintained that he loved me and that he wanted our marriage to stay intact. I felt stuck. We tried to date again but there was too much hurt and bitterness to salvage the shipwreck of our marriage. In truth, it was merely the love for our children that kept us mired to each other. I continued to go through the motions of being the wife and mother, which enabled my husband to believe that since I had just spent the last eleven years doing everything a good wife should do, that I would accept this current inconceivable slap in my face. After his declaration of leaving, I had to quiet my anger and act as if nothing had happened. I made dinner. I set the table. I sat down at the table with my husband and our children as if our world was just the same. I could not bring myself to look at my husband sitting at the other end of the table. I knew if I looked in his direction that I would stand up and throw my plate at his face. That action would end this fairytale that was our marriage.

As a wife, I was finished, but as a mother, I had to hold it together in front of the kids. I did not want to destroy their world just yet. I would put on the brave face to help them. While I had the deep and abiding love for my children, the same could not be said for my husband. Sitting there watching my husband eat the food I had spent time cooking, made me realize that if I had to spend one more second looking at him I might try to run him over with our SUV.

I waited until the children were upstairs and I walked over to him. Quietly and calmly, I told him that I did not care where he went but he was leaving tomorrow. I would not allow him to leave me and then not leave me. I outlined for him that he would pack, find a room, and be gone.
"You will tell the kids tomorrow before you go, why you are leaving," I said with an eerie calm. "You will make it very clear that this is your idea, because I will not have my children thinking that I pushed you out of this house. You want to leave then you will tell the children that you are going and it was your decision to leave."

The next night we sat the children on the couch. They looked at us expectantly. Children are incredibly intuitive and they knew something serious and probably bad was about to happen. My husband told them, "Mommy and I are going to take a time out." I looked at him and wondered at his weakness and stupidity. "Are you getting a divorce?" my daughter asked softly. My husband spewed words out at them. I stated simply, "Mommy and Daddy need to separate to think about some things." I did not want to lie to them because in that moment I knew I never wanted to see my husband again.

Words cannot explain the sadness and horror at watching the two people you love to your core being hit with such painful words. It was as if I were watching someone beat my children and not being able to prevent it. My daughter cried out with such hurt, "No!" My son was quiet. He looked at his feet and said nothing. That scared me! I could feel the pain wiggling its way into their hearts creating significant cracks as it bored deeper into their souls. I knew that this pain would stay implanted deep in their hearts, growing until it festered and they both ended up on a therapist's couch when they were thirty. Yet, I could not stop it. I could not throw myself in front of them as I would if a bus were coming towards them. I could not step in front of them to take all the pain upon myself.

It was undeniable that in that moment I hated this man that was ripping our family apart by his immature and selfish actions. I wanted to hit him so hard that his head would burst open. I wanted to kick him so violently he would cry. As he wrenched apart the hearts of my children, I simply hated him. The hatred seeped into my heart and waited. The feeling of cold, hard hatred knew that I would be calling upon it again. It waited because hatred is patient. It knows that it just need stay still until the day the anger, pain, and fear worked together to create the perfect atmosphere for it to grow. When that day came, it would be ready. Hatred would stand up and wrap its arms around my heart turning it cold and steely.

He packed a few clothes while I stood over him making sure that it was all he took.

"What is this all about?" I questioned.

"Nothing, I just need some time and space," he countered.

"How do I reach you?"

"You can call me on my cell phone if you need me," but it was said with such insincerity that I understood that he did not want me to call.

I lay in bed that night reliving the surreal event that had happened that evening. It finally made sense that our recent family vacation had been more like a week-long game of hide and seek between my husband and me. Whenever I asked my husband to have lunch or spend some time with me, he would send me to the spa or out shopping. While that was a wonderful perk, I knew that something was wrong. I would go looking for him and could not find him. He stayed up later than I did at night working on his computer. He would disappear at a restaurant while we were having dinner with friends. These actions were not in his usual character. Yet, true to the wife I had become, I simply ignored the oddities, and convinced myself that it was my imagination and pushed it out of my heart. I ignored my intuition and was blissfully blind to the flags that were waving in my face.

That night after my husband left, I went about the business of anger and grief. Losing a marriage is like losing a close and well-loved relative. Your marriage is a physical being that has a life of its own. My marriage had become a rather self-absorbed entity. It had gotten too arrogant for its own good. Yet even with all its faults, I still loved the sanctity of being married. I had embraced the quirks and idiosyncrasies that it was made of. My marriage was like an old and worn out article of clothing that I knew did not fit me anymore, but I was loathe to give it up. I kept holding onto the idea and the memory of what the marriage was; and so when my husband left, I was forced to say that this marriage really needed to be thrown out a long time ago.

With my husbands escape, I became the injured spouse. As I put on the injured spouse mantel I decided that I was completely qualified to be a private detective. I spent the next hours and days detecting. However, since I never went to the schools advertised on the back of the matchbook covers, I did not really *know* how to detect. I also did not know what I should be detecting. However, that did not deter my decision to get to the bottom of the bombshell my husband had dropped on me. Armed with only as much insignificant and impractical information that I had gleaned watching *Moonlighting* in the eighties, I decided I was going to find the underlying cause of this enigma and seek out the reason why he had left.

I started slowly by ransacking all available paperwork. I went through bills, home mortgages, and even old glory-day photos of the lying, cheating scum, because I was sure there would be clues to what had happened. I went through coat pockets and dug through drawers looking for something to give me proof, but I had no idea what I was looking for. I just wanted some evidence or some reason as to why this had happened. Why had he left? What had caused this huge act of abandonment to occur?

I was stunned. I was the quintessential deer in the headlights. Actually, I felt more like the damaged and destroyed deer in the rear view mirror after the car had run it over. I had to do something. I could not just sit there in a pool of tears, fears, and abandonment and cry. I had to fight the good fight. I should try to save the marriage, shouldn't I? I had to find the reason that he was leaving. I needed a reason why I was not good enough to make him stay.

"I was not good enough. I was not good enough. I was not good enough." That sentence kept repeating in my head. I had heard that sentence making cameo appearances in my subconscious for most of my life, so it was not an unfamiliar tune. Then the person who promised to love and honor me told me he was leaving, and that sentence took on new meaning. The person I had trusted to always be there and keep the insecurity at bay was gone. I started to flashback through the years of the marriage. All the burned dinners, piles of laundry, and unfortunate fashion choices sped through my mind. For an instant, I believed the words. I am not good enough, and that is why my husband is leaving me. It would have been easier if he had just punched me in the stomach.

That is when I called in the big guns! I called in my friends and alcohol!

Oh, they do not make a tequila bottle big enough. There is not enough award-winning Grey Goose in the world that makes what I had been through better. I could not avoid the pain. I had to slog through the muck of my marriage without boots on and hash over everything that happened in the last eleven years. Thankfully and with much courage, my friends held my hands while I slogged through the hurt, anger, outrage, desperation, and incredulity that seeped up to my ankles. This slogging was going to take anywhere from ten minutes to ten years; it depended on how slowly I was going to walk.

After he left, the days passed, the weeks eked away, and I filled my time with the trivial. I would wash the dishes by hand to take up the time. I was not cooking big dinners with multiple courses anymore, so the task gave me a sense of purpose. Every item of clothing in the house was washed, folded, and put away. My dinners were nutritionally balanced, but boring. Everything appeared in perfect condition. I existed through the days so I could cry my nights away. I would lay my head down on the pillow after surviving the self-imposed monotony of the day and feel the warm tingle begin in my eyes. The tears would start slowly with a few small trickles down the side of my head. Soon I had to bury my head in the pillow so the kids would not hear me. The nights my children were with their father, I rivaled the coyotes outside with the baying of my sobs. I had always been a fun and vivacious person. I played tennis, read books, and enjoyed movies. I loved to travel, experience new music, and maintained to enjoy each day and what it brought; but this loss simply stirred up all the ghosts of insecurity and abandonment that lived in my psyche. Knowing my marriage was bad and wanting more from my life did not stop the fears. The fear that I would not be able to support my children and myself. The fear that I would lose the life I had become accustomed to. The fear of what people would say about me. The fear that I would be alone. Fear, just that, fear.

Even with all the intensity of emotion that I was experiencing, amazingly I started to see little rays of sun outside. I thought, "Okay I am getting better. I will get through this. I am going to be all right. Ha, Ha, Ha!" That was when my husband called and wanted to see if I was all right. He told me he was worried about me. That was laughable. Worried about what? That I was not sufficiently pining for him?

Even with all the anger that I felt, the sadness was louder and stronger. I asked if I could see him so we could talk. He was reticent to come over and I could feel that through the phone line. I told my pride to shut up because I felt so lost. I wanted to talk to the person whom I had spent so much time with through my life. I missed the safety of being with the person who knew me so well. I missed him even with all the hurt, anger, and fear. I missed the safety of us. I wanted back the blessed ignorance that I had had before he left. He arrived at the house; and as I looked at him standing on the porch, I became the stuff I had been previously slogging around in. I was the embodiment of the ooze and muck of a disastrous marriage. I begged, pleaded, and in a moment of weakness, I slept with him just to keep him there if only for a moment. I thought that I could go back to what I thought my marriage was. What I did not realize was that this pathetic, crying person with mascara ringing around my eyes was not that attractive; and if anything, it simply cemented my husband's decision in place.

In what should be the afterglow, I found something else waiting at the end of my bedpost. It was disgust! Oh, I was vile. I was lower than low. I had slept with the person who had just recently sat across from me with his cheat sheets (ah, the irony) and left me. Did I think that this time the sex was going to be so mind-blowingly great that it would heal all our problems and he would see the error of his ways, profess undying love to me, and we both could walk into the sunset together? Yes, I pretty much thought that, even though I was not sure it would be what I wanted. However, this is a real life story not a fairy tale; so what happened was that he left in a hurry, and I sat and cried a few more gallons of diluted Grey Goose knowing that our marriage was indeed over. The bubble of disbelief had been popped with the act of unloving and dispassionate sex. My life as this man's wife was over and reconciliation was not going to be an option for me.

After one sexual reconciliation, I heard a click. I am not kidding, there was actually a clicking sound. I called a mutual friend of my husband's who was like a brother to me; and as we spoke, he foretold my future. He said that it would take a few weeks and I would feel my strength arise. When that happened, I would stand up, get a job, and realize that I was better off. I would embrace my fabulousness; and at that point, I would carry on to find my true self. Once that occurred, I would be strong enough to know that this was the best thing to ever happen to me. That would be when my husband would want me back, but I would not want him. With these words, I came to realizations, epiphanies, and Hallelujahs. I realized that it was not me. He was the one that wanted to leave, so he must be the one with the problem. This marriage was in very deep trouble and the chance of recovery seemed small. With that comprehension, I was able to lift my head off the pillow and come off my liquid diet to eat a piece of toast. It felt wonderful to be alive again. I took a shower and got dressed, and the click got louder. I ventured out my front door to walk to the mailbox and the click got louder still. Each minute of the day that I began to lift my head up, I would feel the pain lessen off my shoulders; as that pain eased, I heard the click getting louder until it actually started to get annoying.

My whole life I had always done what everyone wanted me to do. Being that person, I listened to those that said I should try to work this out. I knew that I could never love this man again after the hurt he had inflicted on my children and myself, but propriety won out. I did not know the specifics as to why he had left, and I thought that I needed a venue that would grant me the ability to extract more information. I suspected that someone else might be an influencing factor but I needed proof. Until I had the facts, I would trust my instincts that told me there had to be someone else involved in this situation. There was a fifty-fifty chance here, so I introduced the idea that we should delve into the world of psychotherapy to solve the why and how-to of our marriage and if we should try to put it back together. The lying cheating scum, as I was so affectionately calling him now, was either going to be one-hundred-percent behind this idea or one-hundred-percent against. I knew that if he was against the idea, then I may as well save my alimony because he was gone and we needed to make funeral arrangements for our marriage. But if he was for it, then I'd better get ready baby!

Therapy can be a glorious thing when used correctly. I know many people that have had wonderful experiences by talking through all the less than enjoyable parts of their lives. However, sitting in an office while someone who has already left you once, goes and leaves you repeatedly while you pay for it seems a tad masochistic. I endeavored to please as usual and wanted to glean more information, so I went. I sat on a leather couch that my fee to the therapist probably paid for and I listened, talked, ranted, cried, and contemplated throwing up while I divulged everything that had occurred in the last eleven years.

As I sat there on the lovely smelling couches, I heard my husband say I was not thin enough, smart enough, cute enough, not a good enough cleaner, mother, lover (ouch, that one hurt, because I was sure that I was not the one deficient in that category) or not a good all-around spouse. In our therapy session, the hatred that had been waiting in my heart made very vocal appearances. I felt rage at his destruction of our life even with all its imperfections. Rage and fear mixed a potent cocktail and I was ready to serve it up chilled and without an olive. I inquired if there was someone else he was seeing, but no answer was forthcoming. I paid handsomely for this laundry list of my shortcomings and still did not have the information I needed. I left the office and the lying, cheating scum (hereafter known as "LCS") wanted to know why I was being so hostile.

"Good question," I thought. "Why am I being hostile? If the LCS was unhappy and I know that I was unhappy, then why was I feeling the anger? Was I really just mad because the LCS beat me to the punch?"

It was then that my own psychotherapy began – stress on the "psycho" part. Enter the friends and the alcohol again.

My friends listened to me try to brainwash myself that I was better off without the LCS. They agreed with this but being true friends did not offer their opinions. I decided I was going to show him by getting a job, winning the lotto (but not before the divorce or then I would have to share it with him), and finding the one great-looking, sensitive guy left in the world. It was war. I was going to show him that I was going to be the victor in this power play. I was going to come out smelling like success and he was going to just come out smelling.

Congratulations, I had now entered the recovery stage. I was stepping on the road to total recovery. On the day I got dressed and realized that there was a lot of air between my waistband and my waist, I knew I was on the on-ramp of the road to recovery. The day I noticed that the guy standing in line at the coffee store was cute and he did not have a ring on his finger, I was about one mile down the road to recovery.

When the LCS called and I no longer felt the flip in my stomach, it meant I was about two-and-a-half miles down the road of recovery. Just as I thought I was ready to accelerate down this road, I was side swiped.

I was feeling like an emotional punching bag as I was drug back into the hurt and pain to slog around some more. In a separation or divorce, this push-pull of pain can happen in many different ways, but for me it was a cell phone bill. The cell phone bill that had recently been being sent to the LCS's office, made a one-time-never-to-be-seen-again appearance with devastating curtain calls.

The mail came as usual, and I looked through to see what catalogs I had received when I saw the bill. A little voice in my head said…STEAM IT OPEN! Okay so my voice is not so little. I put my *Moonlighting* detective hat on again and started up the teakettle. I am happy to inform you right here, that Lucy Ricardo really did know what she was doing. You actually can quite effectively open a letter without leaving a trace of evidence with an innocent burst of steam. What I could not do was close the bill back up without knowing anything. The cat was out of the bag, or in my case, the cell phone was off the hook.

Staring at me in black and white was proof of the LCS's obsession with someone and her various phone numbers. My intuition had been right. There was someone else. Who it was, I did not know but I was certain it was not a business partner. There were so many calls that my eyes blurred. I could not deny it any longer. I was the statistic. You remember the statistic that was stated in one of those highbrow magazines that a woman over the age of 35 had more chances to be killed by a terrorist than to get married. Were the odds greater if that a 35 year-old had already been married once and then had been left by her husband and now was trying to find someone else to marry her? It was my doom and my reality.

In that moment, I turned in my detective hat for a judge-at-Nuremburg cap. I became the great inquisitor. I set up the lights and just waited for the LCS's sweat to pour. I had to hold my heart in check because it felt as if it was just about to bounce out of my chest. I called the LCS and requested his presence at my kitchen table. Living in his new digs on the other side of town, the LCS found treading the ground of his former home rather distasteful especially since his neurotic soon-to-be-ex-wife was commandeering the conversation.

Once he arrived exasperated and angered, I did not dally with small talk. I hit him with it. I came down hard with my proof and felt assured that there was nowhere this dirty rat could run. I turned the wattage up on the lights and waited for the sweat, but it never came. The LCS had been lying and had gotten very good at it. He lied straight through his teeth and for a brief moment, I actually believed him. I guess the shock at his not spilling all the beans made my brain freeze up; and I thought, "My gosh, he must be telling the truth because he cannot think I am that stupid." News flash to me, he did think I was that stupid. He thought that because for the last few months, he had been playing phone footsies with someone else and I had been none the wiser. To prove how stupid he thought I was, he uttered, "It must be someone else's calls on my phone bill." Of course, to the LCS, it made perfect sense that all the calls that were to legitimate businesses were his, but the fifty or so calls to this other woman belonged to some other cell phone user. As the logic of this statement was settling into my brain my outrage was kicking it right out. Then I spoke the classic, woman-wronged statement, "Do you think I'm a fool?" Well, since I had already established that he thought I was stupid, thinking I was a fool could not be far off.

I realized that the syndicated crime shows, as enjoyable as their bantering may have been, did not give me enough tools to flush out the devious mastermind I was encountering in front of me. I needed help and I needed it fast. It was time to call another woman scorned and get quick advice on how to proceed. I called my friend who had lived through worse than I had because her husband had moved from footsies to first, second, and even third base with another woman.

My friend was ruthless in her pursuit of her LCS and acquired a partner to flush out the lies her LCS was telling her. I met her for coffee and heard the gory details of her adulterous mate. In my head, I was categorizing all the same behaviors that the LCS portrayed. After the play-by-play of her situation, she hit me with the important information I had come for. She told me, "You need Frankie from Jersey."
"What exactly was a Frankie from Jersey?" I thought. "Was it a character on the hot mobster show? Was it a hot dog that only people from Jersey know how to make?" No, it was a *real* private detective. Frankie did go to the school on the back of matchbook, and now he was at my disposal to find out just how much lying and cheating had occurred with my LCS.

It was a frightening moment as I dialed the 212 area code. When I heard the voice on the other line, I wanted to hang up quickly or pretend I wanted to know if they had Prince Albert in a can, but I squeaked out my request to speak to Frankie. When Frankie came on the line, I spilled my sad tale. I am sure that Frankie was quietly adding up the cost of a new Mercedes as he listened to me. He was ready and willing to charge up the batteries on his video recorder and follow the LCS around like a modern day mobster Allan Funt. He rattled off his services and charges, as I sat on the other end of the phone at my defiled kitchen table thinking, "How did I get here?" I asked Frankie the question that I am sure he had been asked more than a million times, "Do you think he's telling me the truth?" I realized why the most successful private detectives come from Jersey. "No," he said. That was it. It was out in the open, and I could not fool myself anymore because Frankie from Jersey, the authority on infidelity, had informed me that the LCS was not telling me the truth. So, I settled on a relatively cheap phone tap and called it a day.

That day was fraught with extreme and intense emotions. One minute I was thinking there was no way that a man I had lived with, had children with, and endured eleven years of his boring stories, could do this to me. The next minute I thought, "That lying, cheating, scum…I am going to rake him over the coals!" It was a schizophrenic, out-of-body experience that no drug could help with. After this colossal infidelity accident, I was sent back to the starting line of the recovery road. Having made progress before down the new life highway, I was sure that I could find the express lane to help me back onto the road to recovery.

I decided that it did not matter with whom or what the LCS had been chatting. It did not even matter that I did not know exactly what had happened between the LCS and the mystery woman. The point was that he *was* with someone besides me. He was talking about his problems with someone other than me. He was sharing his thoughts and feelings with someone that was not me. Even if he was truthful in saying that nothing physical had happened, it was still infidelity. The LCS had had an emotional affair, which honestly hurt more than a physical affair ever could. Sharing emotional intimacy and conversation was more of a violation than being intimate sexually with another woman. I realized that if I had not steamed open the phone bill, I might never have known what was going on with the LCS and that there was another person in my marriage.

After this revelation, things started falling into place concerning our marriage. I recalled the times LCS was supposed to have been home and he had been late. I thought about the time he had traveled and I did not hear from him until three in the morning. The slurred excuse of watching a basketball game in the lobby bar had worked at the time because I had trusted him then. It was only now that I understood that lobby bars in hotels do not stay open until three in the morning. I knew that after this enormous breach, there would be no time when I would ever trust him. The trust, honesty, and belief that where he said he was going to be was actually where he would be had been shattered. For this girl, not being able to believe in him was the kiss of death to our marriage.

What am I to do?

At this juncture of my separation, many different things could happen. There could be a reconciliation. There could be more therapy followed by more therapy capped off by more therapy. There could be a parting of the ways. There could also be the decision that after three months of single parenting, I decided I needed to run away from home. I needed to get out from underneath all the mounds of anger, pain, hurt and stress that had been heaped upon me by the LCS. I needed to get away from my home to decide what I was going to do. A spa treatment at a resort was not going to massage away my situation. A night in a great hotel was not going to dream away my pain. I needed to distance myself from the hurt. I needed to be where no one could reach me. I wanted complete and total dissimulation from this event in my life. I wanted to breathe again without the restriction of pain. I wanted to smile.

I ran far away from home. Now the great thing about running away from home as an adult was that you actually have somewhere to run to and the means with which to get there. When I was young and I wanted to run away from home, I would pack up my patent leather red suitcase with one hairbrush and a pair of shoes. Great planning don't you think? Why did I only pack such items for a lifetime on the streets? Because I knew that my mother was never going to let me leave the front door and that I would be safely eating cookies and milk within twenty minutes of my attempt at emotionally blackmailing her.

The LCS, out of the goodness of his guilt, decided that he would give me his air mileage so I could run away in style in business class. Not being one to upset the apple cart of acrimony, I took him up on his offer and booked a ticket to Italy. Unbeknownst to me, the other woman he had so carefully chosen to end our marriage with had told him she was not interested in pursuing their relationship. The LCS figured I was the cheap date scenario of separations. "If you take what's behind door number one, an all-expense-paid trip to a foreign country, you can come back and have...ME!" What he did not understand was that I had boarded that plane months ago. I was already separated from our marriage by an ocean, a few mountain ranges, and several cases of Grey Goose.

This escape was not to emotionally blackmail anyone, except maybe myself. I was running away to a wonderful European country where men pinched all women and the wine was cheap and good. Why you might ask? Because I could! There were people that held me irresponsible for leaving my children and the LCS, to go and cavort around with hot-blooded Italian men. At this point, I did not care what anyone thought. I needed out and if the LCS was going to offer to aid my great escape, then who was I to complain?

The interesting concept was that the LCS thought that if I went to a foreign country alone, one of three things would happen:
1) I would eat lots of pasta and get fat,
2) I would miss him so desperately that I would overlook the

incredible violation he had just carried out against our marital vows and return to his waiting arms, or

3) I would be so guilty at using all his frequent flyer miles that I would simply stay with him. I think he might have been a bit disillusioned as to how valuable his frequent flyer mileage was.

I packed my suitcase and made my escape. As I touched down in Venice, I thought, "I am a free woman in Italy… now where the hell do I find the water taxi?" Not the intelligent comment you might have been looking for, but accurate nonetheless. The fear at trying to finagle myself around Italy with such remedial language skills was lessened as I was able to not only find the water taxi, but also procure one that landed me smack dab in the lobby of my hotel. However, as we are learning in this story, nothing come without a price. My price was 80 euros, which is about 92 American dollars. Yikes, that hurt! I figured as it was my first time to Venice, I should splurge.

Approaching Venice was a wonderful experience, even in the frigid cold of November. The city sits on the water and looks as if it has either just sprouted up from the depths of the sea like Atlantis or settled down on an air mattress in the Venetian harbor. The buildings are old, sagging and cracked, but this is exactly what gives Venice its charm. As I neared the city, a grey mist hovered over everything. It created an impressionist painting effect making all the sharp lines softly muted. It was ethereal and beautiful and I felt my heart soar with the adventure to being alone just beginning.

The incredible vastness of how old Venice is creates awe in cultural youngsters like Americans. Most Europeans, and probably most of the world, view America as the ugly, well-endowed stepsister. Americans have so many desirable qualities, but for some reason we insist on wearing them all at the same time which screams out to everyone, "Look at me!" This over-accessorized attitude is what both fascinates and repels almost everyone in the world about America. We are such a loud, boisterous, cranky child of a country, that most other cultures feel that America needs a good swatting and to be sent to bed without any supper.

My hotel was located very near to St. Marks Square which was truly the heart of Venice; and because of this advantageous location, it was inherent that the lobby of my hotel be opulent. There was gold and crushed velvet everywhere with a guard standing over my luggage while I checked in. Maybe needing a guard to stand over my luggage should have been a less than reassuring fact. A group of attractive Italian men standing in the lobby uplifted me. They were beautifully dressed, perfectly groomed, and speaking the romantic cadence of Italian fast and furiously. I wondered if they were hotel guests or if the hotel had just hired attractive Italians whose job it was to set the female tourists' hearts to beating. I never saw any of these men eating breakfast in the hotel; therefore, I believe that they might have actually been a figment of my romance movie saturated brain. Once I got upstairs to my room, it was apparent that the owners of the hotel had definitely broken the bank with the decorator downstairs and had to do early Spartan flavor in the rooms upstairs. I did not care; I was in Venice, Italy. I was ready to float on a gondola while being serenaded by a handsome gondolier.

Venturing into Venice for the first time, I was surprised at how incredibly cold it was. Nevertheless, I was romance driven to the core and I found a café, ordered a wonderful espresso, and let the Italian romance begin to stir. What ended up happening was I paid eight euros for a cold cappuccino and only an old man with no teeth smiled at me - not a very auspicious beginning.

The next day boded much better. The sun came out, the water was sparkling, and I was ready to walk and view the incredible art that surrounded me. While soaking the history through my pores, I toured the Doge's Palace. The Doge ruled the city of Venice in the days of old and his palace was part legislative hall and part amazingly adorned rooms that he and his entourage lived in. The famous Bridge of Sighs that every tourist that ventures to Venice has a photo of is actually a bridge that prisoners were transported through to the jail across the canal from the palace. The sighs were not romantic in nature but more resignation to an unhappy fate that awaited them. I explored the vast streets of Venice. I walked by a gondola or two. I examined the paintings in the Academia, which is the premiere art museum in Venice. I watched the pigeons attacking people in St. Marks Square with bemusement. The square has so much history. Napoleon found it breathtaking when he arrived. Ernest Hemingway sipped whiskey at the squares outside cafes. Yet, with all the history saturated into the buildings of the square, the most vibrant frequency was the tourist gift shops. Row after row of stores selling the same Venetian glass, watches, or anything that can be sold for double its price surrounded the ancient square.

While it was wonderful during the day, the nights were hard. At night, I would call my children and hear their sleepy voices, because with the ten-hour time change they had just woken up, and my heart would constrict. I would want to zap through the phone lines to be sitting next to them as they hugged me. Instead, I would make myself get dressed to go to the dreaded dinner alone.

It was funny how I needed to go so far away to ease into the concept of being alone. At home, I was not ever truly alone as there was always the dog, the kids, the house, the friends, the stores, the LCS. It was easy to pretend that life without a marriage would not be that different while I was there. In a foreign country, I was truly alone. I walked alone because it was not possible to strike up a conversation with the person standing next to me. I ate alone because I did not bring anyone to eat with. It was a new world that I was moving into. It was the right way to learn how to be completely by myself. I was self-reliant and I enjoyed the peace that came with only having one individual to be responsible for. It was all me for 24 hours a day and 7 days a week. This was a concept I do not believe I had ever truly been comfortable with. Being alone was never an enjoyable moment of individuality in my life. Being alone for me had always meant that no one wanted to be with me. However, in that small café while eating my dinner, I understood that being alone was a gift.

I also realized that I could get royally ripped off in Europe. For example, at the small café which was next door to a small café which was across the street from a small café, I paid almost 62 American dollars for pasta and fish dinner with a glass of wine chaser. For the first few days, I was absorbing the whole European experience and I believed that being ripped off was part of the whole package. I signed the bills and further propagated the whole myth by going shopping for souvenirs.

Venice was where I had my first experience with Italian men. Actually, I believe he was originally from South America somewhere, but he had lived in Venice most of his life. His name was Pedro and he walked up to me and asked if I was American. I, the quick thinker, ignored him thinking that maybe he wanted to retaliate on me for the European Community's wrath at America. I smiled and kept walking. He kept walking too. It was apparent that part of being alone meant that this type of experience was going to happen to me. People would come up and talk to me and that meant that I would have to be able to converse with these individuals. This guy seemed okay; and because of his size, I figured that if he got smart I could probably take him. I stopped walking and told him I only spoke English. He was so excited to learn this fact. I mean, he was *so* excited to speak English. I know this because he must have told me about twenty to twenty-five times. He was sweet and he showed me where the real Venetians eat and drink. The glass of wine that at my evening meal had cost me five euros, cost me only one euro in his neck of the woods. I was learning. I must find where the locals eat and that was where I should eat too. To get to that neck of the woods, we maneuvered through alleys, streets, and over countless bridges, I never would have found the location on my own. I was glad I had a guide to lead me back to my hotel or I would probably still be wandering around the canals of Venice.

A few glasses of wine later, I found myself walking over the Rialto Bridge with Pepito, my little South American/ Italian friend. I was having fun. The lights were shining on the canals and people were talking while sitting at cafes. The cold, crisp air was swirling around me, and I was beginning to feel that perhaps living in a place like this might be the answer. Yes, why not run away forever - was that possible? Then the truth crashed in on me. Where I was enjoying the fun and camaraderie of my newfound friend, he was look- ing for a completely different type of friendship. I made my excuses and had him show me the way back to my hotel.

After two days in Venice, I was more than ready to leave. I was ready for some sun and smiles. Venetian Italy was not the Italy I was used to. Venetians were more staid in personality.

Being merchants and businessmen for so long had taken the frivolity out of their Italian nature. I figured they must store up all their fun for the carnival season. I wanted the animated conversations and the pinching-bottom Italy. I wanted the ochre buildings and the azure sky. I wanted to eat gelato while watching old men play bocce ball. I needed to head south. Dragging my suitcase over several of the lovely Venetian bridges to the train station I was ready to head to Florence. I managed wonderfully at the train station and was quite pleased at how easy it was to get myself aboard the train. Yet once on the train and in my seat, I was stymied as to why the "destination" said Roma. I must have asked every Italian walking by the train, in the train or close to the train, if I was on the correct train. Finally, after twenty-one "yeas" and one "not-so-sure," I gave up the fight and decided I would get there if I was meant to. I started to think like an Italian right there.

I arrived in Florence and I stepped off into the Italy that I knew and loved. It was loud with everyone talking and gesturing with their hands. The sun was out and stores were open. Vespas (mopeds to us Americans) were buzzing around like flies. It was like coming home. I felt instantly right with the world. I hailed a taxi to take me to my hotel. Since I had dark hair, dark eyes, and gave directions in my limited Italian, the taxi driver assumed I was a local girl. This assumption worked to my advantage for the entire trip. I was never over-charged by taxi drivers nor accosted by the Italians selling leather, because they believed me to be one of their own. I also never had my bottom pinched either, something I had actually been looking forward to. Deposited at my charming hotel, I was excited to see that it had a rooftop garden overlooking the Ponte Vecchio. This bridge was simple but its history was not. The Ponte Vecchio had been used by the Florentines to cross the River Arno since Roman times. The bridge housed many shops across its span during its existence. Now the stores are mainly jewelry stores and their prices are reserved for the bravest of tourists. After unpacking, I quickly left my room and made for the Uffizi Gallery only twenty steps away. There art history heaven was waiting for me.

The Uffizi is nothing to look at from the outside, but inside is the most impressive art collection per square foot. The only museum that comes close is the Louvre in Paris. The art is phenomenal. The beauty and the artists whom I saw as I perused the walls, truly boggled my mind. To stand in front Botticelli's Venus and look at the brush strokes was a bit disconcerting. This work of Venus, naked and rising out of the sea in a giant shell, was ever more vivid in person. Many of the works I saw are in the media all the time. The paintings of the masters like Renoir, Picasso, and Van Gough are used today to hawk cameras, cars, and even copy machines. The over-saturation of these masterpieces tarnishes the idea that the paintings are great works of art that a genius put on canvas several hundred years ago. As I stood in front of these paintings and felt the age and beauty radiating towards me, it seemed to put everything into perspective. A man or woman took a brush, dipped it into paint they had made, and applied the color onto a canvas. While it seemed a rather mundane itemization of actions, they had created emotions for millions of people who looked at their work. On every wall in every room there was magnificent art, and I drank in each piece I looked at. The Uffizi was an incredible experience.

The other magic of the galleries was that I was never completely alone. I could be lost in my own space, yet surrounded by others. This transition was the subtle process that I needed. There were crowds thronging to see the wonderful works, and there was the age and the stories behind the paintings themselves. As I stood there in front of even the plainest of pictures, I could feel the history of the painting hitting me square in the face. Every painting had a story. Those stories were sitting and waiting for me to stand in front of each work and feel the story unfold. As I stood looking at the images before me the history would sit on my shoulder as I admired the beauty. Every painting had a vibration. Some works I walked past barely noticing them. Other works I would stand and stare at for long periods of time. One room housed floor to ceiling tapestries that depicted a young girl's whole life story. The tapestries did not look like fabric that had been weaved. Instead, the colors and patterns exhibited shades that seemed like they had been applied by a brush. I wondered about the craftsmanship and how something of this caliber was never created today.

Time had no meaning while I was alone. Being alone meant I did not have to hurry to make a tour bus. Alone I could stand in front of any of the works for as long as I wanted without anyone looking at me as if I was crazy. Alone I could absorb everything I wanted and nothing I did not want. Surrounding myself with all that beauty was the best way to ease myself into being alone.

Night in Florence was an experience of light and noise. On my first night, it was the passegginata. This is a stroll that takes place around nine at night until people feel like going home. It seemed as if every single person who lived in Florence was out walking on the street. I walked along looking at the people as they talked and laughed. Families were out even though it was ten-thirty at night. Everyone walked, talked, shopped, ate, and enjoyed life. I felt this was a lesson Americans could learn. We should get out more, walk around, and interact with each other. No one seems to be alone in Italy. They know the people walking toward them. They know the people in the cafes. Italians live life mingling with the lives around them. They have a daily ritual of walking down the same streets, seeing the same people, and building long-lasting relationships with each other. I felt enveloped in the warmth of friendship and joy.

Florence brought many joys to my trip. Santa Croce, the cathedral that houses Michelangelo's grave was stupendous. An American girl, who was studying in Florence, gave our group a guided tour. It was wonderful in two ways. The tour was fascinating with all the history of the church, and it was wonderful to speak English to someone. Our guide also gave wonderful restaurant recommendations. I ended up eating at the little café she had recommended two nights in a row before I was embarrassed to go back because I thought the wait staff there would be wondering, "This lady can't find another restaurant to eat in anywhere else in Florence."

I walked across the Ponte Vecchio crossing the River Arno and climbed to the top of a hill to the Piazzale Michelangelo. The Piazzale is above the city and from this vantage point, I could see how large Florence really was. I sat eating delicious gelato and watched the sun turn the ochre and burnt sienna paint on the buildings to incredible vibrant colors that exploded and transformed their exteriors. Looking around at the mix of tourists and locals was entertaining. I do believe that might have been the best gelato I had the whole trip. That is saying a lot because I consumed a lot of gelato!

No visit to Florence was complete without ogling *The David*. Everyone knows this statue. All women *know* this statue. This sculpture must have caused much heartache in the women of 1504 after it was unveiled in the Piazza Vecchio. Imagine that you are married to just a run-of-the-mill guy, and then they unveil *The David* and you have to go home to *The Guido* every night. It must have been very upsetting for the Donnas (translation is "ladies" in Italian) of the day. I stood looking at this statue in astonishment. To think that Michelangelo was able to cut with a chisel and hammer through a piece of marred marble that no one else wanted and created such a work of perfection. The sculpture was beautiful and fallible. The proportions appear off with the hands and feet too big for the body, yet it all works together to create a perfect balance. After spending about three hours in front, behind, and to the side of *The David*, I thought that it was going to be hard to find a flesh and blood sculpture to erase that image out of my mind.

As the end to my time in Florence drew to a close, I was sad to be leaving and excited to be heading for Rome. I anticipated seeing all the wonderful sights of Rome and to experience staying right above the famous Spanish Steps. There was a sadness that came from the knowledge that I only had three nights left in Italy. Little did I know that they would be the three most exciting nights of my trip.

Arriving in Rome was a new assault to my senses. The volume seemed louder in this city. The people were dressed beautifully and with such style. I can thankfully say that the sweat suit craze that has swept the American nation has not reached the shores of Italy, and hopefully, never will. Nothing was more attractive than watching an Italian man in a beautiful tailored suit walking down the street. Lucky for me, this vision occurred quite frequently in Rome. I was whisked off to my hotel by a taxi. When I arrived at the hotel, my room was not available for me to check into yet. With wonderful Roman charm and hospitality, I was brought to the roof garden, given a cappuccino, and assured that they would send someone to come and get me in ten minutes when the room was ready. An hour later (let me introduce you to Italian time) I went down to the front desk, and amid "Mi scusi" which was the Italian way of apologizing, I was escorted to my cozy room. It was beautifully appointed, and I wish now that I had been able to spend more time in it. Are you intrigued?

In Rome, the Italian experience further came together with shopping. I shopped at a boutique where I bought some beautiful sweaters that will feature later in the story. Then I made my way to the Roman Forum. I walked on the same streets that Julius Cesar, Marc Anthony (not the singer) and Caligula trod upon. The age and history of this place was overwhelming. Entire buildings still stood from Roman times. Needing to hear more history about this incredible location than my guidebook could give, I attached myself to a tour with an English-speaking guide. The tour further enhanced the experience of walking through this ancient city. From the tour guide, I learned that their company offered tours guided by American students studying in Rome. I signed up straight away for the walking tour of the city offered that night.

At 5:30 PM, after crossing traffic that would frighten most New Yorkers, I found my tour gathered in front of the Forum. The cast of characters were: Josh, our very young and impressionable tour guide; two wonderful and fun girls from a liberal arts college in South Carolina; a quiet but lovely woman originally from Russia, but now living in Palo Alto, California; and myself. I was beside myself to find people to speak English with, and even more excited when before we had been together five minutes, we had already decided that we would be dining together after we finished. Josh had his hands full on this tour! Once we began walking, we all enjoyed the wonderful facts that Josh was able to provide for us. When we reached the Trevi Fountain, Josh informed us that there were three wishes available for our choosing. If I threw three coins in the fountain, I would be coming back to Rome. I had done that when I was eighteen and here I was, so it must work. If I threw four coins, then I would meet my true love in Rome. Not a bad deal either, I thought. Finally, if I threw five coins in the fountain, then I would meet my true love, get married, and live in Rome. Good concept but not entirely practical for me, so I settled on four coins and having a great love. I mean, that is a pretty, cheap price to find the love of your life…right?

After our tour, the girls and I found a quiet Italian café and ate a delicious dinner. We drank lots of cheap wine and enjoyed its desired effect. We all shared our stories of love, laughter, and loss. By the fifth bottle of wine, I believe that we were even too loud for the Italians at the café. For me it was bliss to laugh and joke in English and share in good ole-fashioned American camaraderie after seven days in virtual silence. With our last bottle, three Italian men who also had heard our raucous laughter, joined us. They, of course, had already imbibed their requisite bottles of wine, and we seemed to all be on the same level of intoxication. They wanted us to join them at a dance club not far up the street. After inhaling some wonderfully decadent gelato, we hurried off to our rendezvous.

The dance club was quite a sight. A transplanted Chicago boy of the rougher variety owned it. He had long white hair, tattoos, and wore a black motorcycle vest. He looked tough, but was sweet; and his wife, Vette, was the bartender. It was a family-type nightclub. He had brought the acquiring of junk to a new level. There were more items hanging on the walls than I have ever seen before in one place. Even in the collectors' heaven of the States, this place had outdone itself. The bathroom was a feast for the ocular senses. It was based on the old-fashioned toilets of Europe with just two holes in the ground that you stand above to do your business. However, this concept was not as appalling as it would have usually been, because there was so much madness occurring around you. There was a small lagoon filled with water with a sign posted that threatened attack by a crocodile if anyone got close. There were Christmas lights and flashing strobes hanging about the loo that created a crazy idiosyncratic barrage against the senses. All this insanity enhanced with alcohol made for a twilight zone type of experience.

Out in the main room filled with Italians was a DJ playing a cross between jazz and disco. Dancing in the middle of that fray were three uninhibited and slightly inebriated Americans. Since I fit that description, I was, of course, front and center in the mad gyrations considered dancing in this club. There was only a five-by-ten foot dance floor, which was more like a dance *postage stamp* than dance floor, therefore, making fluid and attractive movements was seriously hampered. Not to be intimidated by a lack of space, the three Italians were swishing us all over the floor. My friends and I were doing our best to keep up, but at times, we nearly missed landing in the lap of the throng crowding the edge of the dance postage stamp. It was fun, frantic and everything that you would expect in a nightclub in Rome.

From the dancing and continued beverage consumption, there came the spark of attraction. Alex was tall, brazen and Italian, need I say more? He grabbed me by the waist and spun me into oblivion. I was drunk with not only alcohol, but also the frivolity of the moment. Alex made me laugh. He was a lawyer whose favorite phrase was, "may I speak to you the truth?" I told him countless times that I wish he would. By two o'clock in the morning, more truth had been told than I probably needed to hear. Alex, it seemed, was a collector as well. His collections were the girls of the different continents. It seemed that he had a German girlfriend, a Swedish girlfriend, an Italian girlfriend, and I believe I was auditioning for the banner of American girlfriend. He was charming and sweet, but I took nothing he said seriously, of course neither did he. He walked me back to my hotel while we laughed and told each other what it was we really wanted out of life. I am sure that at that time of night and with so many draughts of wine in my system, the idea of working as a part-time film critic for the *New York Times* seemed a perfectly plausible job description for me to aspire to. He was an attorney who wanted to be anything but, it seemed. He kissed me goodnight; and it was sweet, tender, and exactly what I needed. As I said goodbye to Alex, I thought to myself that my Italian journey was now complete. I could see the Vatican tomorrow and go home entirely happy. That was when it hit me that I had forgotten my three new sweaters in the club. Upset more at the loss of the sweaters, which I quite fancied, than the euros that I had paid to procure them, I believed that they were history. It being four o'clock in the morning, I fell asleep quite quickly dreaming of Louis Armstrong being sung with a heavy Italian accent.

Waking up on a bright November morning with the knowledge that many ounces of Italian wine were still coursing through my system did nothing to hasten my ability to get out of bed. Slamming my hand down on the sleep button countless times, I finally mustered up the gumption to fold the blankets down. From there the progress was slow but steady. I was due to arrive at 9:30 AM, at the newspaper stand located near the Foot Locker in front of the Vatican Museums. I was meeting our group to tour the Museum and St. Peter's Cathedral for the day. I was excited but a bit hazy on how I was going to manage the intensity of the day with less than three hours of sleep. The promise of staring at the Sistine Chapel spurred me into a pace a bit faster than a sloth, and I managed to get out the door with enough time.

Taking the Spanish Steps faster than I probably should have, I headed for the Metro station. As I entered the station, I figured that it would be an easy ten-minute journey on the train to one of the holiest places on earth. However, I did not realize that getting to a holy place requires the exact change. I had no option other than to walk like the pilgrims of old to the Vatican City proper. Now having to get from one side of Rome to the other is no light stepping task. To get there in less than half an hour called for someone in peak physical condition. Realizing that I was far from peak condition but rather in a more *peaked* condition, I hunkered down and set off. To say that it was a brisk walk is a bit of an understatement. At one point, I may have passed a Vespa or two. Finally, there was the sight I had been searching for, the Foot Locker! Huddled under the sign, looking not much better than I, were my two friends. We each found it amazing that the other had made it here. We recounted the events of the night before with much laughter. We had all experienced a connection of being other Americans in a foreign place, and the need to sightsee just further cemented our relationship.

As we stood in line for the Vatican Museum, we were buzzing about seeing the Sistine Chapel and all the glories that were in store for that day. Security is tight around the Vatican as you can well imagine. We were frisked and poked; and finally, we made it through to the inner courtyard. Our guide was great and filled with little known facts that make taking a tour entirely worth the cost. We saw phenomenal things in the museum rooms that led to the Sistine Chapel. The Raphael rooms are actually a misnomer, because only one room had actually been painted by Raphael. An incredible artist, he died suddenly at thirty-seven and the gossip was that the death was caused when he contracted syphilis. I am sure that made front page of the ancient gossip magazine.

The beauty and abilities that surrounded me as I walked through this ancient place caused a sort of electric buzz in my body. It was almost too much to take to look at all this very important art and know that I would have to remember every bit of it in my mind because photos were not permitted. I searched the walls to etch in my brain the incredible scenes I was seeing. My brain, meanwhile, was working overtime with a hangover to try to catalog all that the retinas were sending its way.

As I huddled outside of the entrance to the Sistine Chapel, my anticipation was palpable. I knew that I was about to look at a masterpiece that is the basis for all masterpieces. I was about to look at Michelangelo's *piece de resistance*. It is interesting to note that Michelangelo did not want to paint the Sistine Chapel. He was forced, by the Pope of the time, to paint the chapel. Michelangelo had other ideas and fled to the countryside to hide. The Pope had to send troops to go and find Michelangelo in the small town where he was hiding and drag him back to go to work on the chapel. After that dramatic scene, Michelangelo spent two years working on the chapel. This fact does not make any sense. How can someone create such a magnificent work in size and in scope in only two years and under duress as well? The amount of story, color, and inspiration in this great work was beyond comprehension.

An interesting side note, it was commented on that Michelangelo loved his orange, knee high, suede work boots (artistic, wouldn't you say?) so much that he didn't take them off for any reason for the almost two years that he worked on the Sistine Chapel, pause for the cumulative, "Ick!" When he finally finished the chapel and decided to take off the boots, they had attached to the skin on his feet. I guess in Michelangelo's case, cleanliness was not next to godliness. Anyway, when his valet finally was able to pry the boots off, part of his skin came with them. Okay, I know you are saying, "Why is she sharing this story?" Well think about it. You are an undeniable genius in art, architecture, sculpture, and color but you cannot remember to take off your boots at the end of the day. I found this story such a character statement of one of the greatest artists of all time.

The time came for us to enter the Sistine Chapel. It was explained that there was no talking in the chapel because it was a very holy place. It is the location where they choose the new Pope when the previous one goes on to meet the holiest one. The ceremony is shrouded in secrecy. No one is allowed in the Vatican City during the assignation of the next Pope. Security is key and the various Cardinals are sequestered in the Sistine Chapel until a decision can be reached. Each day the votes are burned in the fireplace and the puff of smoke that emits from the chimney tells the awaiting crowd if there is a new father of their church. Black smoke emerging from the chimney means no decision has been made. If there is a white puff of smoke then the celebrating begins. Given the sanctity of this ancient tradition, I understood the motive behind not being able to take photographs in the chapel. Yet this holy tradition is not the reason; it is purely commercialism. Damage to the art from all the flashes is not the motive, instead it is that Nikon Corporation owns the rights to all photos taken of the chapel because they financed the restoration work done on the Sistine Chapel in the last few years. Take a moment to digest this. One of the most priceless, beautiful, and incredible works of art is off limits because a Japanese company owns the imaging rights. I wondered if I had a Nikon camera, would that have enabled me to take a picture. How would they know anyway? Is there a Nikon employee skulking about, just waiting to jump out and yell, "Stop, put that camera down?" Further pondering, if the Pope wanted to take a picture of the chapel would he have to get permission from Mr. Nikon?

Once we entered the chapel, I was at first struck by how dark it was and then by how loud it was. For a place where talking was not permitted, it was droning pretty loud in there. As I contemplated this fact, I heard an incredibly loud clapping sound followed by, "Silenzio per favore!" (Which in English is: "Silence, Please!") The clapping sound was echoing off the walls and most people were stunned into momentary silence. I looked around to see where the loud applause was coming from and saw that there were about ten Italian guards in the room and their sole job was to clap and silence the crowd when the "no talking" got too loud. I wondered if these guys ever got tired of saying the same thing. I wondered if occasionally they didn't just want to say, "Yo! Shut up!" As is to be expected when you have a room full of tourists, the noise level once again reached high-drone mode in about five minutes when the previous attempt to silence us was reenacted.

To try to explain the fantastic sights that I was exposed to in the chapel is to struggle with the adequacy of words. I started from one side of the chapel and continued to the other side. I was forced to keep my neck craned to see all of the ceiling. Amazingly, even though it was so high above. The colors and the definition seemed to jump out at me. The crowning glory had to be the hand of God. The picture seen countless times in print was more undeniably beautiful in person. The poignancy created by the almost touching fingers of Adam and his maker was the true relationship of all people to their God. The spark of life that God gives Adam is awesome in its simplicity. Barely touching fingers with God creates the vibration of life in Adam. The beauty of the blue sky that frames the figures of God and man was perfection. Michelangelo truly gave us a piece of Heaven here on earth with just that scene. Every scene that was on the ceiling was as breathtaking as the next. The front wall of the chapel depicts "The Last Judgment," it is the portrayal of man coming before God to recount their sins. All manner of awfulness was depicted. Death, dishonor, pain, and strife was amazingly and accurately etched in the faces of the lost. Michelangelo painted skin melting off of bodies, animals biting the limbs of the damned, tears and fear frozen on faces, and still there was a beauty to the work. For someone who can barely draw a stick figure, to see the total perfection with which Michelangelo created his works was remarkable.

We left the Sistine Chapel and moved onto the other parts of the museum and my brain began to overload. It was as if seeing the Sistine Chapel was the cutoff for my grey matter's absorption capabilities. Everything that followed, as ancient and perfect as it was, was gravy for my wine saturated brain. Items stuck out here and there; such as, the candlesticks that used to light the Apian Way in Roman times, the statue that looked like Bill Clinton, and the incredible bowl that Nero used to float flowers in on his dining room table that probably could have held my Toyota Sequoia in it. Those items my

brain opened up for briefly after the Sistine Chapel. Nevertheless, once we got to St. Peter's Cathedral, my brain had gone
out for pasta and a cappuccino.

After the tour, we decided that sustenance was a necessity.
We had walked for just under six hours. With weak and wob-
bly knees, we managed to find a café that fit everyone's price,
choice of food, and ambiance needs. We had acquired two
more individuals to our modest group, a couple from England
who were warm and friendly. We enjoyed our meal with them
and invited them to dine with us that evening, but they were
heading home early the following morning.

It was then that the black veil started to close in around
my eyes. My body said, "SLEEP, I MUST HAVE SLEEP!" I
knew better than to argue. My partners in wine agreed that
they needed to sightsee a bit more before we ate again, so
we made a rendezvous to meet at seven o'clock that evening.
Remembering my beloved sweaters, I asked if we could eat
somewhere near the previous night's debauchery, so I could
look in at the nightclub and see if my sweaters were sitting
around having a beer.

Walking back to the hotel, I tried not to knock anyone
over or kick any random dogs, as I was a bit cranky. As I fit
my key into the door of my room, I barely made it to the bed
before falling into a deep and dreamless nap. Three hours
later, I was raring to go. I was newly outfitted and wearing
highly impractical suede shoes. I managed by accident to
find the actual piazza where we had met the night before and
waited for my friends to locate it as well.

Standing there taking in the atmosphere around me, I
almost pinched myself for the disbelief that I was standing
in Rome after enjoying such a spectacular day of sights. I
saw my friends winding their way towards me. We hugged as

they recounted the three hours more of sightseeing they had achieved. I notated the fact that they were just, "so young." I laid down the gauntlet; did they think we could find the nightclub that we had been at the night before? They wondered why, and I told them my sad tale of forgetting my newly acquired, favorite sweaters. We hunted and searched and miraculously, we found the place. Unbelievably, it was closed! Friday night in Rome, and the club was closed? My friend stated the obvious. In a city where most people do not consider dinnertime to be anything earlier than 9:30 PM, why would a nightclub be open now? We decided that we would eat dinner first, and then come back to our newly acquired stomping grounds to visit my sweaters.

Dinner ended up being happy hour in a pub-like bar that offered free food and a menu of drinks that would have kept us busy for days. I decided, when in Rome with college girls and I chugged on a Long Island Ice Tea. Several of those later, we decided that we were ready to go on the search for the sweaters in the infamous nightclub. By the grace of the Roman god that was patron to slightly intoxicated tourists, we found the place. The incredible part was that they not only had my sweaters, but also remembered us from the night before. Wait, maybe it is not so hard to believe that they remembered us, given our Dancing Queen moves on the dance postage stamp. I called out, "Let's celebrate!" and proceeded to don one of the wayward sweaters. (In the psychotic bathroom of course; I was not that inebriated.) One of my friends decided that two late nights in a row would put her too close to edge of death's door and opted for a cab ride back to her hotel. My other new friend said, "Order me up one of those frothy strawberry things." Spoken like a true tourist on the edge, we sidled up to the bar and began a long relationship with our bartender, Vette. She was making drinks that would have made Emeril proud. There was plenty of *Bam* in her cocktails. After several of these wonderful libations, my friend and I realized that we were being relocated by the manager of the bar. He kept moving us down the bar towards the door until I asked him if we were going to be drinking al fresco. It was then that I saw the reason for our recent migration. He was tall, dark, and handsome. His eyes were soft and warm, and he was hunky in a way that made my knees weak. I looked at him and thought, for this I can move.

Amore for me!

Since he was sitting right next to us, it only took a small amount of time before my friend and I were conversing with Nicco. He spoke English quite well and in a bar with loud music, it sounded perfect. I think the *Bam* cocktails might have helped with the translation too. Whatever it was it was all working. I found myself smiling, flirting, talking, and probably all of the above too much. I was enjoying the attempt at conversation, and I was thinking, "Can we move this entire club to California, because my mojo really works here."

Nicco was there with his cousin and his cousin's friend. These two individuals deserve further description. It was a Mutt and Jeff type of partnership. They looked like identical twins where one had been given a growth hormone and the other not. They both had shaved heads. They were dressed almost identically, but with enough differences that they did not look like their mothers had called each other up and planned their son's attire for that evening. They did not fit with Nicco.

Nicco was classic and smooth. He was refined. As we conversed, I learned that he was a lawyer and that he did not live in Rome. He lived in a town on the sea near Naples. He was thirty-nine and loved movies and books. Too soon, he and his cousins moved to leave. I smiled and believed that our fleeting flirtation was coming to a close. Then he asked with incredible forthrightness, "Would you like to go out with me tomorrow at eleven? I answered quickly, "Yes," and just like that, it was settled. He wrote his phone number on a piece of paper, and I told him where I was staying. Then he left.

I must admit I was a bit let down that he was leaving so soon, but I hoped for the best and that I would actually hear from him again. I did, and sooner than I had hoped. He came back into the bar and asked where we were going, and I informed him of our plan to find a disco that an Italian waitress had told us about. He told me to call him at one o'clock, (now this is in the *morning* mind you) and he would come and meet us. Then he was gone. Well you can imagine the conversation that occurred after he left…lots of "Oh, my gods," and "He is so cute," being bantered around, mostly by me.

My friend and I finally felt that we were ready to find the disco that was located on a street, on a corner, somewhere near the bar where we had had dinner. Armed with these very concise directions we made our leave. The walk was fun, cold, and filled with laughter. I decided that since I had met someone, my friend should share in the same experience with me. I pointed out men on every corner to find one that might spark an interest; but alas, when she finally saw someone she found intriguing, he turned out to be an American. Oh, that will not do, I thought. She must have a romance. You cannot have a romance with an American, while you are in Rome. This particular American put me off because he asked if I was my friend's mother. I have been called "ma'am," and the first time that it happened, I felt a constriction in my chest. However, I do not believe I have ever been considered a twenty-two-year-old's mother. As the outrage started to boil, I realized that I *could* actually be her mother. I mean a very young and hip mother, but her mother just the same. That hurt. It felt like someone had slapped me. I looked old enough to be mistaken for a college girl's mother. Someone bring me the Botox shots and Retin A, Pronto! Being the forthright person that I am, I promptly told the young idiot that there were two things you never assumed about a woman: 1) that she is pregnant, and 2) she is someone's mother. Sure that I had given him a practical lesson that would help him throughout his dismal life, I moved on to matchmaking him with my friend.

After our brief conversation with foot-in-mouth-boy, we decided to continue with the disco location project. Forty-five minutes later, we had passed by the same Renault four times, and everything was starting to look a bit foggy. I determined that it was nearing the hour of one a.m., and I was going to give my Italian lawyer a call since finding the Holy Grail of Disco Dance did not seem like a viable option.

As I dialed the phone number, I panicked, what if he didn't remember me? Of course, I probably should have thought this through before I dialed the number; but by then, the phone was ringing and someone was saying, "Pronto." I broke into very fast American. This was a language very different than English. This was the speed talking of one who was either nervous or had drunk too many double espressos. I was racing through my description about who, what, and where I was when he said, "I will meet you now." I was glowing and floating; and I am not sure if that was the alcohol or the handsome Italian I was rendezvousing with. Whatever it was, it was bliss. If I could have bottled that feeling, I would be a billionaire in about twenty-five seconds. My friend and

I floated, well *I* floated and she held onto my ankles, as we made our way back to the piazza. I still remember seeing him walk towards me. It will be one of those memories that visit me often throughout my life. His strides were long as he came towards me. He smiled, and it made my heart soar. His face was beautiful and strong, and I was ready to let fate take me wherever it wanted. It was too much like the romance movie that seemed to always be looping itself through my brain, yet it was real. I could not believe my luck.

We all walked to a bar that was noisy and bright and also made frothy, fruity drinks. Unfortunately, or maybe fortunately, these drinks were missing the *Bam* of the previous cocktails. Because of the volume in the bar, it was necessary for me to sit very close to Nicco as we talked. I learned that he was divorced and had a son. Nicco was in Rome to help his cousin with contract negations for his business. As he talked, I watched his beautiful green eyes and stared at his hair that called out for me to touch it. Our legs touched as we sat there and I think we were both happy for that.

My friend was finally crashing and needed her hotel as soon as possible, so Nicco called his cousin to come and pick us up to take her home. She was leaving for Florence the following morning, so we hugged goodbye and promised to write, email, phone, or fax, to stay in touch. She disappeared into her hotel, and I was alone in a car with three unknown Italian men. What is a girl to do?

They were going to another bar and asked if I would like to join them for a drink. "Why not?" I thought. I mean at this point, "Why the hell not?" I had unknowingly bought an E-ticket ride on the drive-thru-Rome express. The wild rides of American amusement parks had nothing on this. We took off at a speed of 60 miles an hour and that was the slowest we drove for the next twenty minutes. The speed would have been okay if there had not been hairpin turns and switch-backs occurring about every minute or two. I was being tossed around the backseat like one of those bobble-headed dolls. Thank goodness, Nicco was there to catch me or I might have bounced right out the window.

It was then that the voice started in my head. This voice sounded a lot like my friend from home. We had seen the recent movie about the divorcee who went to Italy, bought a villa, met an Italian man in Rome, got into his car and drove with him over four hours to his house to have dinner. Safety seemed to have gone the same way as time had in Italy; but interestingly the plot lines were similar to my story, except buying the villa part, but the night was still young. Anyway, my friend had said to me in that darkened movie theater, "Don't you dare do that." I recall my answer, "I would never do that." Well, the best laid plans.

Meanwhile, we were jetting down the road and I noticed that there was less and less city to see outside my window. I began to think, "I am going to die." I was going to be found on the side of the road somewhere; and the person who found me would think, "Who is this girl, and where did she get that cute sweater?" Feeling a bit of panic, all that came out of my mouth was 'Dov'e?" My limited Italian left me with only the ability to ask, "Where is…?" I kept repeating this statement, over and over, when Nicco reached out and took my hand. Suddenly, the panic settled and I realized that I was safe and unbelievably in the exact place I should be.

I settled in for the ride that was taking shape, and I must educate you of another advantage to the Italian man. They stop and ask directions! It was a bit of bliss right here on earth to see these strong and macho men asking everyone how to get to their destination. I was smiling a rather Cheshire cat grin that baffled my compatriots, but trying to explain the reason for my grin with my limited skills in speaking Italian would have been too time consuming. After what seemed like an eternity on this Italian rollercoaster, we finally screeched to a stop in front of a dark building where people were coming out two by two. After a brief discussion, we learned that the sought after bar had just closed. Then round two of the wild ride of Rome started. Back we went and I saw sides of Rome, I don't think most Romans have seen. It was thrilling fun, and I loved every minute.

Nicco and his cousins were speaking hurriedly in Italian that I was enjoying listening to when we screeched to a stop and Nicco and I got out and into a taxi. We made our way back to my hotel and he walked me to my door. He kissed me on the cheek and told me he would call me tomorrow. I walked as if on a cloud (I finally knew what this hack-neyed expression meant) to my room. I swear I was buzzing from the nearness of this man. It was a wonderful feeling. I looked at the clock and saw that it was nearly three-thirty in the morning. I was certainly getting my money's worth in this hotel.

At ten-thirty the next morning, Nicco called and we made plans to meet outside my hotel and go have coffee. I got ready and waited with mixed feelings. I was nervous and excited and anticipated…what? I did not know but I knew that this was the beginning of another wonderful memory. When he arrived, he kissed me on both cheeks and we began our day of talking. We stopped for coffee and talked the whole time. We discussed movies, art, our lives, our dreams, and pretty much everything else in between. It was wonderful to be sitting in Rome at an outdoor café with a charming and handsome

Italian who could speak English! I was in a grown-up Lizzie McGuire movie.

Nicco and I walked through the streets, and when he reached for my hand it felt as natural as the ground under our feet. We walked and talked. I learned that he loved to shop. He loved to play European football. He missed his son and proved this fact by dialing a number on his cell phone. He held the phone to me, and I listened to the sweet voice of his son on the other end asking his father questions. Nothing could have endeared me to Nicco more. To watch a man speak to his child with such open and unspoiled love can be a powerful thing.

We ate lunch outside at a café and talked even more. It was heaven to have this much conversation with a man. I did not have to pull it out of him. He was asking questions and actually listening to the answers. At one point, he even asked me, "What are you thinking?" I thought I had died and gone to heaven. After lunch, he had to go to do some work. I was planning to go to a museum and visit the Coliseum. He walked with me until there was no more time left, and then he kissed me and said he would call me later so we could go to dinner. My skin was electric and I felt a buzzing in my chest that I did not believe I had ever felt before. I walked in one direction, and he walked in another; and I felt pulled to look back at him. As I did, he turned and looked at me and we both smiled. It was as if we both felt, at that moment, the exact same thing. It was a wonderful and blissful feeling that I hope I never forget and hope that I find again.

I settled back into my routine of art and walking. Yet this time, the walking was enhanced with remembering. I encountered my first Italian protest while walking to the Coliseum. It was interestingly enough not a protest for Italy but a protest by El Salvadorians wanting freedom. It was loud and crazy. Yet with all these people protesting loudly down the street, the Roman people were walking in their high-heeled shoes, beautiful clothes, and ignoring the protest while they talked. Once I reached the Coliseum, I was awestruck by how high it was. I thought how impressive this must have been in its glory. Even if the events inside the location were a bit horrific, you could not deny the grandeur of the building. Again, the age factor came into play as someone whose country is only hundreds of years old stands and looks at this ancient building still echoing with the cries of gladiators, the growls of animals, and the prayers of sacrificed Christians.

Once I was back in my room, I sank down on my bed for a bit of respite when the phone rang. It was Nicco and he was finished with his work early and wanted to know if I wanted to meet him. I asked for fifteen minutes and I would be down. As I got ready, I felt that I could not stop smiling. I never thought about what would happen later. I never thought about where this would go. I only enjoyed the moment and the joy that it was bringing me. It was a pure and wonderful feeling to just experience the moment that we were in. It was simple; I was going to enjoy myself and pack this wonderful experience in my bags and bring it home as a souvenir.

I turned out of my hotel and saw Nicco turn down my street and I smiled. We walked into the throng that was night in Rome. We walked and talked and then stopped for a drink and talked more. Sometimes, the conversation was disjointed as we both tried to explain an idea to each other. At times, we just gave up and laughed instead of exhaust ourselves with too many words. As he took my hand in his, it felt right and safe. His hand was large and warm and with my hand curled up in his palm, I felt so beautiful.

We stopped to eat pizza for dinner. Nicco swore that pizza was not good unless it was from home. I swore that pizza was not good unless it was Round Table. Neither one of us believed the other on that fact. We enjoyed our meal, but there was a bit of sadness surrounding the night because we knew that tomorrow I would leave and this bit of magic that we had found would be gone. At one point at dinner, I felt him staring at me and I asked what the matter was. He said that he was just making a memory for when I was not here anymore. I understood that idea.

As we walked back to my hotel after dinner, Nicco stopped and pulled me to the side. He looked at me and then lowered his lips to mine. At first, it felt strange and awkward to be kissing him, but then as he encircled me in his arms, our lips found the right rhythm and it was joy and imagination at the same time. We kissed like teenagers. We would walk and talk and then stop and kiss some more. It was one of the most romantic times in my life.

It is my belief that American women are attracted to European men because they still have the gift of romance. The men in Europe still believe that a woman should be touched, caressed, and cherished. They understand this because their women demand such attention. In America, women have created the demise of romance all by themselves. We want to be treated equal with men. Do not harass me sexually, or I will sue you. We can do anything a man can, and watch me do it. All these battle cries, while they are empowering, have decimated a man's ability to find a woman vulnerable and sweet. Men have forgotten how to let us know that we are important, special, and just so necessary to their lives because we have not allowed them to feel that way about us. If they call us terms of endearments that we do not like, we tell them. If they bring us the wrong kind of flowers, we tell them. If they do not do something in the bedroom that we insist on, we tell them. We are so busy telling them what they are doing wrong that we have completely forgotten to tell them when they do things right.

Men have given up the fight. It is too hard and demeaning to try to do something special for a woman and find that it comes up lacking again and again. At some point, men decided, "Why even try; because I will just fail again." The romance gene dried up in men in America, because it was unused. It withers and dies because of neglect. In reality, American women have no one to blame but themselves for the lack of romance in their lives. We women still *need* romance in our lives and because we are upset that at home our man is not sweeping us off our feet, we flee to the theaters to movies that are so impossibly romantic that you can get a cavity just watching them. These films spit out what we women are missing in our real lives. After watching these unrealistic and completely contrived stories of love and romance, we go home where we are thoroughly and completely let down by the man that romance forgot. It is a vicious circle and one that would end if we all stopped trying so damn hard to be the tough "I-am-woman-hear-me-roar," and just let our natural, soft, and beautiful essence come out.

In America, we have an epidemic of plastic surgery, fad diets, bulimia, anorexia, pills to pop to make us feel better, and doctors to talk to that can fix our psychosis and neuroses. Everyone looks to the outside of our selves to make our lives better. Women think, "If only my breasts were bigger I would find a man who would give me the romance I need," so these women run right out and get those new and improved breasts, and for a while they are happy. For a while, they feel right with the world. The men come, they pay attention, and for a time the woman is satisfied. The woman feels it must have been the big boobs, because she had never had so much attention before. Eventually when the men are not paying as much attention as before, the woman goes out and gets a tummy tuck. Again, she feels wonderful, happy, and beautiful. The men come back and the woman is happy. Are you getting the pattern here? The surgery does not make us more attractive, it is the attitude. When the outside remodel of the new and improved version of ourselves is done, we believe that we are better. We hold ourselves with renewed confidence. The bigger boobs or the flat stomach did not attract the men; they were attracted to the inner glow that comes from a woman who feels confident in herself.

The sad thing is that the surgery is not necessary for any woman to feel this way about herself. Sometimes in dire cases where there is disfigurement or extreme distress, then surgery is a blessing. However, the way many women from the age of seventeen to sixty are jumping under the surgeon's knife is a pathetic way for us to behave. Women should be confident because we are special. We should be confident because we are warm, inviting, and smart. We should be confident because when we love a man, we love him wholly and completely. This *should* be our surgery, to cut out the doubts and fears that make us unlovable in our own eyes. If we could do that, then no one would ever need fake breasts again.

Back in Rome, the romance continued. As we were walking, Nicco told me that he wanted to come and visit me in the States. I smiled and nodded thinking that by tomorrow night I would probably be a distant memory for him. As we neared my hotel, I felt torn. I wanted to stay with him but I had an incredibly early flight in the morning and I had to get some sleep. As we climbed the Spanish Steps we stopped to talk and kissed some more. I put my hands through his hair and pushed it out of his eyes. The emotions that I saw as he looked at me, I felt in my heart. I was doing the impossible for me by simply living for the moment. I was soaking in all the energy of this moment to use later as a memory. It was a sweet memory that I believed would help me to get through many a hard time to come.

Finally, I could stall no more, and I had to go into my hotel. I told him how wonderful meeting him had been. He smiled and kissed me goodbye. I waited until he got into his cab and then I walked to my room. The glow that followed me there kept me immobile for a time. I lay on the bed just letting the energy flow around and through my body. As I lay there, the phone rang. Nicco was calling to say goodnight and to tell me to think of him tomorrow. I told him that I already was thinking of him. I kissed him once more on the phone and let it go.

The alarm clock going off at four o'clock in the morning was as violent as being slapped across the face. All the warmth of my dream-filled sleep was yanked right out of me. I finished the last-minute packing and ventured out of my room. The whole of Rome was sleeping. I thought back to the previous nights, when I had just been coming back to the hotel at this time of the morning. The journey back to reality was beginning.

Driving to the airport, I looked around at the sights that were now dark and deserted and wondered when I would be back here again. I wondered what my life would be like then. I wondered if Nicco was dreaming of me. I could not wait to see my children and have their wonderful arms around me. It was bittersweet like all beautiful memories are. As we neared the airport, I knew that the whole trip and especially the last few days had been an amazing and important gift to me. The strength that comes with traveling across a foreign country alone gave me a sense of wellbeing that I had not often felt. I could do anything at that point. I had spent ten days meandering across a foreign country with no mishaps. This gave me courage and a sense of confidence that was rejuvenating. I knew that these ten days would never leave me; and someday when I lay on my deathbed, I would be thinking about my time alone in Italy. I could still feel Nicco's kisses on my lips, which created a joy that was bounding in my chest. Those feelings would keep me going once I arrived home.

Wishing there was more

Flying home from an adventure is much different than flying to an adventure. The unknown is a powerful thing. The known can be just as powerful. I spent much of my flight reliving the night and day before. Over and over, I could feel the joy and warmth of setting the scene in my mind and playing it, then rewinding it and playing it again. It was blissful and sorrowful at the same time.

Crossing the miles started to bring me back to the reality of what I was returning to. Waiting for me was a man who had hurt me with lies and deception, a marriage that was in a very bad place, and a life that was uncertain and unknown. This was the not so great flipside of running away. At some point, I had to come back and deal with all that I ran away from.

The captain turned on the seat belt sign and announced our descent. For that moment, I was only thinking one thing; I want to see my kids. I want to hug them, kiss them, and feel their unconditional loving arms around me. I was excited as the plane taxied. I was getting a bit antsy waiting for luggage. I was downright unnerved as I waited for customs. Soon though, I was exiting through the doors and scanning the crowd for the two faces that I loved most in the world. There they were, calling me something that felt so familiar and so true, "Mommy, Mommy, Mommy!" As soon as I heard their voices, they were in my arms and all was right with the world.

On the other hand, there was the man that I had loved for the last eleven years standing there looking as if my coming home should solve all the problems we had before I left. I felt awkward with him. I did not know what to do. I did not know how to approach him. I took the coward's way out by fixating on the kids and throwing out comments to the LCS over my shoulder. This worked pretty well all the way home as I told the kids about my trip and showed them pictures. I gave them small gifts to appease them until I could get home and extract their real presents from my luggage.

I played the role with the LCS until I got home. Home had become an interesting word. The more time I spent in Italy, the more comfortable I became with it. It felt a bit like home but in a different sense. It was not the home of memories and my history. It was a place where my fear of being alone began to dissipate, and I began to see being alone as a *positive*, instead of a fate worse than death. Italy was home to my crossing of the threshold of who I was going to become. Being there had allowed the "*real me*" that I should be to start to push out from under the "me" I had been before. For that reason, it was home to me. It was where I realized that emotional love and intimacy were absolutely necessary to me to be happy in my life.

We drove into the driveway of my house and everything looked the same. It was as if while I was gone, it had all just stood still waiting. I went in the door and smelled the smell of my house. I saw all my furniture and the colors and everything that I had been away from just rush up and hug me where I stood.

I busied myself getting out gifts and talking so that I could keep my distance from the LCS without appearing to actually be distancing myself. After the newness of my being there was starting to fade and the kids were falling back into their usual life, I heard the phone ring.

I looked at the number and felt my heart began to pound and beat and thump in my chest. It was *him*! Nicco was calling me at just precisely the wrong time and yet at exactly the right time. I ran into the other room and picked up the phone. I said hello and waited for the international connection to go through. He said he knew that this probably was not a good time to talk, but he wanted me to know that he was thinking about me. He told me he would call me the next morning at eight then blew me a kiss and was gone. "He called, he called, he called," kept running through my brain. I felt like I was fifteen and my first crush had called me. In truth, it *was* a first crush. It was my first crush as a woman alone. It was the first time in the last twelve years that a man other than my husband had made me feel like my heart was going to explode. It was wonderful. Yet with this wonder came the pain of having to lie. I had to cover as to who it was on the phone and the deception began. Why I felt the need to be so considerate with the LCS, I do not know. I guess I am just a better person than he is.

Eight o'clock in the morning could not come fast enough. In fact, he did not make it until eight. The phone rang at seven, and I came awake quickly as I reached for the receiver. I could feel his smile through the phone lines, and I am sure that he could feel mine too. We talked quickly but with raw emotion. He told me he missed me and that he wished I were there. Amazingly, I wished I were there too. I loved my children and would never leave them; yet at that point, I was not sure where I was supposed to be. It felt right in Italy and it felt right at home. I felt that the relationship that could have been with Nicco had not had enough time to cement. I knew the potential was there, even with all the obstacles, but I was not sure if this flirtation could survive the shallow planting it had received.

During the next few days, I spent most of my time smiling and counting ahead nine hours trying to determine what time of day it was for Nicco. The phone and text message lines were burning up between us. We were averaging about four to five communications a day. Every time my phone would ring or my cell phone would buzz, I would feel as if I was standing right next to him in Rome. My life after I got home was ruled by our unofficial phone schedule. Every morning he would call when I woke up. If it happened to be a weekday, we would talk quickly. We talked more leisurely if it was a weekend. During the day, my cell phone would send me love messages and I would smile from ear to ear. It was bliss, pure and unadulterated bliss. I felt seventeen again with all the butterflies and violins that go with it.

We talked about everything. We shared our likes and dislikes. He talked about the end of his marriage and I talked about the end of mine. He sang to me on the phone and begged me to sing to him. I was shy since coming home, and I did not talk as much as he did. Over the phone, talking was difficult because we did not have each other's face, eyes, or hands to help facilitate our language barrier. However, we succeeded on many different fronts. One day, I was a bit late in calling him when he called with a sense of urgency. I started to apologize for the delay, when he stopped me and told me just to listen that he had something to say to me. He proceeded to tell me that he never felt like this about someone so soon and that he could not stop thinking about me. More importantly, he wanted to tell me that he loved me. I was seriously swooning. The phone was heavy in my hand. He *loved* me? How could that be so? How could this man, whom I barely knew be talking about love? The crazier thing was that I felt that I loved him too. I understood that the feeling I had in my chest was different than I had ever felt before. All the reading that I had been doing regarding chakras and spirituality had fine-tuned the energy in my body. Even though it seemed ridiculous to the outside observer, Nicco's and my soul felt extreme emotion for each other. I threw in my abandon and all propriety and told him that I loved him too. At that moment, as I sat in my backyard feeling the sun on my back, and with his words coursing through my mind, I did love him. More importantly, I wanted to be loved so even with the rapidity of the statement, I allowed myself to believe. I would not let myself think about the "what ifs" and "how can its"; I just allowed myself to be caught in this pure emotion.

Nicco told me that he wanted to come to see me. He wanted to be there with me and to spend more time with me. He was planning his trip for ten days in December and asked if that would that be okay. I looked at the calendar. He would be arriving in just three weeks. I had the kids and everything else that day-to-day life brought, but reality was on the back burner. I just knew that I wanted to see him again, and I wanted it to be for as long as possible. I said yes, and we both got busy making plans. There were many discussions on the phone, and ideas started to grow that we both thought maybe the other one might be "*The One*." We both had the intensity of emotion. We both felt that love could really conquer all. Neither one of us wanted to see that thousands of miles of distance, a language barrier, and the fact that we did not even know each other seep into the fantasy we had woven around us. We were both too happy living in the world of romance.

The phone calls continued and everything seemed wonderful; then it happened. The other shoe dropped. As the week before his arrival dawned, he became ill. He was home in bed for three days and was not able to walk or talk much. I noticed that things were beginning to change a bit. Our phone calls were getting shorter and the messages on my phone were happening less and less. I started to panic. In true inner-child mode, I started accusing him and asking him why he was not coming. I started causing scenes and finding rationalizations as to why he seemed cooler than before. All the insecurities of my past abandonment were rearing their ugly heads. He had to change his flight plans because he did not think he was going to be well enough to travel, and his arrival got pushed back four days. Still I believed with the faith of the hopeless romantic that he was going to arrive. In my head, I would play his arrival at the airport over and over. However, I never could get the image of me rushing up to him and embracing him and that should have told me something.

Meanwhile, I was hiding all of this intrigue from the LCS. I was trying to be a big person and not rub his face in my new, gorgeous, Italian boyfriend. I made sure that he would not have to know that Nicco was visiting and that would save him pain and suffering. Why I was being so thoughtful with the LCS's feelings when he had not been very thoughtful of mine was not a question I could answer. I guess it was just decency on my part. However, even with all my attempts to keep the LCS in the umbrage of my clandestine visit, the truth was set free.

The LCS had been visiting the children. As he prepared to leave, we were talking. It was the usual conversation of "this bill is due," and "please do not come into the house without calling or knocking," when the phone rang. Since it was about ten o'clock at night, he wondered who could be calling. I did not answer the phone, because I did not want to talk in front of him, and the phone stopped ringing. Ten seconds later, my cell phone started ringing, and the jig was up. The LCS wanted to know who was calling so late. The first question he asked was, "Do you have a boyfriend?" I started feeling guilty and began making up excuses when I realized that I did not have to answer to him. I did not have to share this part of my life with him. He was not entitled to know everything about me anymore. I told him to leave and that it was none of his business who was calling. Well honey, I should have just gone and got that red scarf out of my drawer and flashed it in his face a few times. He was on to me now and he then put on his *Moonlighting* detective hat and got to work.

The LCS graciously offered to sit with the kids one night at the house while I went out. Why I did not see alarm bells in my head, I cannot say. When I came home from a dinner out with friends, I could feel a pall hanging over the room. It felt oddly like how I used to feel as a kid when I knew I had done something wrong and my parents were going to ground me. The LCS started spewing facts and telling me that he knew everything. He spilled all my beans verbatim from my emails, and I cursed myself for not hiding them somewhere on my desktop. I felt stupid having bought the LCS's altruistic offer of babysitting. I was not thinking that he had ulterior spy motives, duh! He started accusing me of being unfaithful, stealing his money, being a slut; the list of my crimes was long in his mind. I withstood the attack in awe. We had been separated for over five months, and here I was being harangued by the LCS that I was a fornicator. Fantastically, the LCS would not divulge where he got his information and I quietly stated to him that I knew he had read my email. He countered that statement with, "Well, you read my phone bill." I could not believe that he was saying this as if this was a defense for violating several of my civil rights. Calmly I uttered, "Yes I did, and I would do it again." Since the LCS was counting on the guilt card, this statement caused him to pause. The LCS lost his composure in the face of my calmness. He accused me of having an affair. The fact that he could actually make this statement with a straight face was hugely comical. I sat there not believing my ears since not five months ago he had been burning up the telecom cells with his little phone hanky panky.

Everything went downhill from there on all fronts. While I was fighting off the LCS with his accusations about my character, I also had to combat the barbs that I had stole from him because he had paid for this trip and I had led him to believe that I would be reconciling when I returned. I thought, "Was he on heavy drugs?" I realized in that moment that his master plan had backfired. He had thought that after time spent away from him I would see the error of not taking him back and come running home hoping to reconcile. I will take a moment here for you to pause and laugh. Since the LCS did not know what to do when faced with his plan that been so blatantly foiled, he did the only thing he could do after eleven years of perfecting it, he blamed me.

Meanwhile, not everything in happy-go-lovey land was going well. The romantic calls were becoming shorter and farther between. There seemed to be a tension between the previously blissful romantics. I began to feel that there might be something shifty going on in Italia; but instead of just ending it and moving on with my life I bought into the idea that everything was going to be fine. Then it happened. Nicco stopped calling. It was as if a large pair of scissors snapped the international phone connection to my phone. There was nothing. I started to panic. I thought that perhaps he was sicker than anyone had thought and had to be taken to the hospital. My imagination began working overtime creating a deathbed scenario of doctors discovering a brain tumor in Nicco's head. So now in my crazy world Nicco was in surgery and no one knows where I am or even who I am. Since they can't speak English, no one would think to call me to let me know the dire circumstances of his illness; so there I was, sitting in a wading pool of self-induced hysteria. Twenty-four hours passed, and I could not reach him by cell phone. He was not answering any of the messages that I had left. Finally, in desperation I left one last message saying that I had to know if he was okay and to let me know how he was and I would not call again.

It was the day before my beloved Italian was supposed to arrive when I received a text message at five in the morning. It had only been a couple of hours since I fell asleep because I was preoccupied with worry, so I was groggy when I retrieved the message. Even half asleep, I was hopeful. I felt that I would finally understand the abrupt change on the love front. However, I was woefully mistaken. The message was vague. Actually, it was more than vague; it was downright cryptic. It simply stated that Nicco had been sick and was at home resting in bed. Sick, resting, that was it. That's all I was going get. No explanations, no apologies, no words at all? There was nothing. It was complete incommunicado! Of course, I could not just let that be it, even though I had stated I would. I needed to know what was going on from the horse's mouth. I got up the nerve to call his home in Italy and hoped Nicco would answer and not his scary mother. Who was I kidding?

If the guy was not courageous enough to call me and tell me himself that he was not going to be coming to visit and that everything had changed in his heart, then he certainly was not going to answer the phone when a heated up, worried American girl called him. His mother answered, and I was just able to get out some semblance of understandable Italian. There was a slight pause as the gruff-voiced mother spoke to someone. Then incredibly, as I sat there with my heart in my throat, the phone was set back down into the cradle. I had just been hung-up on, internationally. I stood there for a moment struggling to conceive of the fact that someone had just dissed me long distance. I was angry and wanted to blame everybody in the entire world, especially NATO because they are blamed for everything. However, the only one to blame was me. I was devastated, yet probably not completely surprised. I was definitely hurt, and that hurt just kept on getting bigger and bigger until I felt like a weight was on me. Did I not just go through this with the LCS?

At this point, I had to bow my head in shame and call my friends who, by this time, had Grey Goose chilling in their freezer. Many mimosas later, after we had dissected and picked the bones of my relationship clean, I realized something very important. Going to Italy to find out how to be alone does not mean that I should have hooked myself up with an even more unavailable man to create a dream relationship with. I started to see this for what it really was. This was a lesson disguised in a very nicely groomed, Italian wolf's cloak. Whether there were true emotions on Nicco's part was not the point. The point was that I went to Italy for answers, and I got them. Those answers were to help me to continue on my path, but the answers were not supposed to become the question. I needed to take a step back and know that coming home to a broken home and marriage was a hell of a lot easier to take when I had a handsome Italian professing love to me. The relationship with Nicco also helped to keep me strong enough to learn that emotions, romance, and true love were things I was *not* going to live without in this life. What Nicco offered may not have been the true and right thing, but what meeting him did give to me in even the smallest amounts was the resolution that being in a marriage that was just okay was not good enough for me.

Unfortunately, this clarity did not stay with me all the time. There were many pockets of time where I cried, wailed, and uttered, "What happened?" There are so many differences between men and women, but one very vast one that I have never understood is a man's inability to end a relationship when it is dying. It seems that anything they can think of would be a better use of their time…walking the dog, cleaning out the filters of their heating ducts, getting their teeth cleaned…than simply standing before a woman and telling her that they "just aren't that into her." Men are desperately, undeniably and utterly afraid to face a woman about to be scorned. What do they do when faced with this horrific task? The only viable action they can do is to run and hide. When I say run, I am not talking about a pleasant jog around a high school track, I am talking about a full-out sprint with no looking back to see if you are gaining on them.

Most men I have encountered become deaf, dumb, and blind when they want out. It would not matter if I walked up and popped Nicco in the nose; he would have pretended it had not happened and kept on walking. This ability is one that causes much confusion in women. I do not have this erase mode in my brain chip. I need closure. This word is very important for women to move on. We NEED to be told, preferably to our face, that the relationship is over. If I am not told that the guy and I are finished, then in my mind the relationship never really ended. This relationship will be stored on the shelf awaiting reentry by the person who left. Like a Twinkie, the relationship has an uncountable shelf life.

I knew a woman whose boyfriend never called her back. He just stopped calling after they had been dating for a while. This was a love of her life type relationship, and I am sure that she spent many days in the Grey Goose haze of "Why me?" After an appropriate grieving period, she got on with her life and her love life. Flash forward two years later, and she is walking down the street when her cell phone rings. Calling was the boyfriend of two years before, who simply says, "Hello." What happened here? Did he just pop out for milk two years ago and end up on the side of the carton instead? What made him think that after pulling a Houdini trick on her that she would even want to talk to him? I wanted to know what he had said. "I hung up," she told me. I could not believe my ears. She hung up? I mean this was a monumental situation. This was the moment every woman who has been walked out on, waits for. She had a responsibility to women everywhere to get some answers. She needed to cause this man to sweat. She needed to find out for all of womankind why he, and in a roundabout way, all men acted in this manner. She hung up! I was astounded and a bit in awe.

After hearing her story, I realized that I had joined the throng of women with missing men that belonged on the side of a milk carton. My milk, or should I say latte, was beginning to curdle. Time was going by, and I accepted that I would not be hearing from Nicco again. Still I held out hope. I formulated questions in case he ever did call and folded them into my wallet so if I happened to get a call on my cell phone two years from now, I would be ready with my interrogation. I would know the how, why, what, and where of this relationship's demise. I would have my answers. However, the silence continued. The times of day that used to be so magical, now were just times of the day again. It became second nature for me to look at the clock and see the hours passing, and not hear the phone ring. Worse still was when the hour that with Nicco in my life was so exciting came and the phone would happen to ring, I would run to the phone hoping against hope that his number would show up, but it never did. I had to try very hard not to sound too disappointed to the person calling me on the other end.

Time went by and I would fight my brain to stay away from the memories. Those same memories that had been so precious now felt more like poison. It seemed like everywhere and everything I saw reminded me of him. I would hear a song, words spoken with an Italian accent, or even a commercial for the Olive Garden, and I would want to break into tears. My whole adventure was tainted with heartache. Even the wonderful memories of the beauties I had seen, were marred by the hurt that was emanating through my body. I could not even develop my pictures from the trip because it hurt too much. I was driving my friends crazy, and they were running out of Grey Goose. They started to buy Smirnoff now.

The day that Nicco had been going to arrive dawned, and I forced myself to stay busy and try not to think that I should be driving to the airport to pick him up. It was futile. Every minute, I thought about where we would have been and what we would have been doing. I kept staring at the clock and feeling the pain to the tips of my toes. It was bone crushing, and I had brought it all on myself. Why did I promote this impossible dream? Why did I not just leave the improbable situation in Italy where it belonged? Because I had made it real, I needed to go through the real pain that it created. Finally, I could not take it anymore. As the holidays came upon me, I sent an olive branch message that was very non-threatening and wished him a Merry Christmas in Italian. I did not expect a response, but I felt better knowing that I had at least put a friendly ending to our story, not such cruel disinterest. I was wholly surprised when I received a text message on my phone with Nicco wishing me the same holiday wish. Did I dare to hope that perhaps he was thinking about me too? I waited, thinking certainly he would write again or call, since I opened up the door and left it ajar. The words were brief, and once read, they were gone. It was time for me to admit defeat. The relationship had departed; or in my case, it had been deported.

Now I began to get angry. I started by singing songs in the car telling Nicco how much I hated him for hurting me. I began to listen to country music, because let's face it, they write the best songs for people hurt by love. I tried to hold in my tears and put on a brave face because I knew that everyone believed that I had set myself up. I could not understand how a person that had told me he believed that I was the last love of his life, could then just erase me from his memory, thoughts, and actions. It seemed like an unfunny prank that God was playing on me. I did not want to go to the place where I doubted my own abilities to see when someone was not telling me the truth. I wanted to believe that I was a better judge of character than that. I felt that if I were honest, then they would be straightforward as well. While these thoughts made me feel very vulnerable, I struggled to believe that while this pain was so real now it would not always be like that. I slowly began to feel better in small increments. It became easier to recall aspects of my trip and not feel the stabbing pain in my heart. I began to talk about what I experienced on my trip without having to get out a new box of tissues. I looked at the photos of my trip, but I could not quite look at Rome yet. I found myself healing. It is said that for every month a relationship lasts, it takes that many weeks to heal. Given the short duration of my love tryst, I figured I could grieve two-and-a-half weeks, tops. As time passed, I started to laugh at jokes. Hearing the word "Italy" did not send me to the ladies' room to recoup. One day I became conscious of the fact that I had not thought about him for most of the morning. I was coming into the sun. I had survived the tempest in my damaged life raft, and I was going to be rescued. How that happened was up to me.

I'm still alive

The healing began in earnest. I read all the self-help books I could get my hands on. While on this journey of self-discovery, I heard myself spewing spiritual healing tricks to my friends. Everyone thought it might be time for a healthy suggestion like, "You might enjoy getting a job." What they were really saying was, "Get busy and leave us alone, because you are driving us crazy." I think that my friends believed that I was going to show up next time they saw me wearing a saffron robe with the smell of incense wafting along behind me. One friend even said, "You are starting to scare me." With these words of worry in my ears, I transitioned from the self-help cycle and made up my mind up that it was time to begin the life that I had been postponing during the last eleven years. The time had come for me to begin again. I had come face to face with the "*real me*" and she was a strong, capable, idea-filled woman that could do anything she set her mind to. I had refreshed my mind, body, and spirit so now I needed to put it all together to get myself back into the land of the living. The question was how to do this?

I was lucky and my wonderful, dear friend told me about a job that would be perfect for me. I went for the interview, and that afternoon I had a new chosen profession. I was working in an office learning the hotel service industry. I might not have picked this career myself yet it was exactly the place I needed to be. The job filled my days, and long hidden aspects of me started to re-emerge. Other coincidental events made it apparent that everything happened for a reason. People that I met and issues I was going through were all part of a plan to show me what I should really be doing here on this earth. I was here to learn about *who* I was, and how what I did affected those around me.

Lessons came in many different forms. Some lessons were quick and brief and learned in only a moment. Other lessons could take years and years to make themselves known to me; and when they did, I still might not understand their purpose. Other lessons were unbelievable and would probably make no sense to me until ten or fifteen years down the line when if I was lucky, I would have an "aha!" moment while getting my car washed and it would all fall into place. Whatever way these lessons were going to come to me, I was going to see them as the gifts from the spirits and energies that rule this world. I had been given a special dispensation to learn these lessons here, and I was going to make the most of it. By letting go and giving the issues and problems to God and the powers that be, it took away the stress of thinking that I had to fix it alone. I could just go along waiting for the universe's answer to my problems or questions. Often the answer came faster than I could ever imagine. Through the losses I had encountered, it was apparent that I was here for a reason. I believed that my reason was to meet and interact with other individuals while teaching and learning from them. When I allowed these pains and growths to arise in me I was also feeding the energy of the world flowing along with me. By giving of myself, I would make my life better. By learning to help others, I would learn what could really help me.

The other part of healing was learning how to stay busy. While my job kept my days busy, I needed to find a way to take up the time of the nights. I decided to join a singles group. The organization set up three men and three women together to have dinner. It seemed like a low-pressure way to meet new men, develop friendships with single women, and experience a nice night out. I knew that if I did not have some sort of social schedule, I would either go out of my gourd or become a professional hermit. I did not want that for my future, since the pay was probably not very good. When I signed up, I was asked to write a list of qualifications that I wanted in the man I hoped to meet. My list of what I wanted was long. My list of what I did not want was even longer. Filling out the forms, I had to go over onto the back of the sheet and the coordinator of the group might have had to bring in a few more reams of paper to attach to my file. I took time to think about what I really wanted in a man. It was like making a shopping list to go grocery shopping except someone else was going to be squeezing the fruit for me.

On my first foray into the single set, I chose a New Year's Eve party. I figured it would be a celebration and would be an easy way to dip my toe into the dating pool. I headed into the city where I had booked a hotel room knowing or hoping this was going to be a raucous night out. My friends were incredulous and made comments like, "You're so brave," and "Aren't you scared?" I figured after spending time cavorting through Italy by myself that to make it across the bridge to a party should be a piece of cake. It was a cardinal rule in my experience, that if I expected too much I would be let down. That being the case, I decided that I would have no expectations regarding bringing in the New Year. However, once I stated that I had no expectations, things kept popping into my head. Let's be honest, what I wanted was to walk into this party and lock eyes from across the room with a wonderful, tall, beautiful man that would whisk me into his arms and tango me across the dance floor. He would whisper into my ear that I was the most beautiful woman in the room and he had been waiting for me his entire life. Then he would move me to the edge of the crowd and ask how he could make the rest of my life blissful while he kissed my hand and fed me chocolate… oh, excuse me, I drifted off for a moment. As you can see, I was having no preconceived ideas about the evening. When I arrived at the venue for the New Year's Eve extravaganza and checked in for the event, I was seated near some people that looked as if they were having a good time. I drank my complimentary champagne and started up a conversation with the person sitting next to me. I had a very good time that night. I made friends with two nice girls and decided that this was another part of the puzzle that needed to be fit together in my new world as a single woman.

When I was married, all my friends were married with children, as I was. I mirrored the life I had with the friends that I formulated. It was not that I could not have single friends, but my comprehension of their lifestyle was not as understanding. With friends similar to me, there was sympathy if I could not leave the house for a week because my kids were sick. My friends that were married could relate when I had snapped and served my family franks n' beans because I just could not be creative in the kitchen one more night. Our lives were parallel, so friendship was easy to form with them. When I first became single again, my friends made sure to invite me to come with them and their spouses to dinner parties because they were empathetic of my situation. I was struck with the fact that I did not fit into that world anymore. I was the odd woman out. It made me feel even more pathetic that couples were looking at me with "poor her" stares. I still had the kids, so I was not a pariah on that social level. I had always been very active in my children's lives. I belonged to the PTA, worked in the library, and helped out in my children's classrooms. I planned fun and exciting birthday parties for my children and brought cupcakes to school to celebrate the day of their birth with their class-mates. I was actively involved in their after school activities and made sure that I knew their friends as well as their friend's parents. My children knew that I loved them with all my heart and was there to support their lives. This part of who I was, never changed or was questioned. I was first, and foremost, a mother; but as time went on it became increasingly clear that my married friends did not want me around. Perhaps it was because not only was I a glaring example of how separation and divorce can happen to anyone, I think they also begin to worry that I would start asking their husbands to come over and unclog my sink. Suspicion seemed to become rampant. One close friend coldly stated to me that she could no longer trust me to be around her husband, especially if there was drinking involved. I looked at her with surprise and incredible hurt as I asked, "Who are you more concerned about, me or your husband?" While that shut her up for the moment, it ended our friend-ship. The new title of Ms. in front of my name had put me in the position to have to find a new place to socialize where I did not make so many people uncomfortable.

Here is where I began the adventure of being single once again. I knew I was entering a new and uncharted world as a later-thirties divorcee. In my twenties, I was able to go to bars and enjoy the pseudo-glamour of the cool bar and the cool men and the cool ladies and the cool bartenders. I felt that I belonged there, and it was my *right* to flirt and party all night long. However, dating in my late thirties was extremely different. There were different camps populating the bars today. There was the divorced woman making a re-emergence back into the dating world. There was the never married thirty-year-old that was still dating; and of course, there were the twenty-year olds that made all the rest of us cringe whenever they walked into a room. It was not that I felt less attractive than they were, because I knew I had attributes that the twenty-year-olds did not have, but they had the trump card; they had youth. I decided as a divorcee, I could be either very bold or very timid about how I re-entered the dating world. If I chose to be bold, then I could go to a bar and sit by myself and have a drink without batting an eyelash. I could chat to any and everyone, and people would be taken aback by my strength, independence, and self-confidence. I never got that bold. However, I did have a different attitude about this new ritual of dating. I was not going to care. I went out to be with friends and we enjoyed ourselves by making our own fun. Sometimes a man would catch my eye, but I did not go out just to meet someone. While that would have been a nice bonus, the friendships and the bonding that we were doing was the focus of our excursions.

My new single friends were starting over too. Some of them had been dating and going through the growth process of divorce longer than I had been, and they held valuable insight to what I was about to experience. Other of my friends were just getting their toes wet with dating again, just as I was, and we valued each other immensely as someone to hold onto so we did not drown. Being supported in this manner, combined with age and wisdom, gave me a new strength in the dating realm and I wished that I had been this strong when I dated in my twenties. Often times, this new attitude was just what the doctor ordered and I met and dated many men. However, I needed to keep in mind that if I was dating men that I met in a bar, I was interacting with a certain type of guy. A man that came to a bar to meet women was often looking for a certain type of behavior to occur that I was not willing to enact. I began to see that men my age were talking and flirting with the twenty-year-olds. The men that looked like my father were chatting me up. One night after too many old men wanted to whisk me away to Hawaii on their yacht, a light bulb shone above my head. The illumination was dim but the wattage it packed was strong, and I cautiously decided that I needed to not be hanging out in bars. It is hard to find a location to date once you are over thirty and doing beer bongs was not an option for me. While there were so many women like me out there, I found that we all seemed to have the same woeful questions about how to meet quality men. Since no one appeared to have an answer, I just went where everyone else went. Something was better than lonely.

There are unwritten rules for women over the age of thirty-five. For example, a rule would be that over the age of thirty-five, I should refrain from wearing blue nail polish. That was a rule I could live with. Another rule was at a certain age, I would need to cut my hair to shoulder length as anything longer would not be seemly. I do not know if I agree with that rule. Then there is the rule that at a certain age, I should not wear what I saw in a fashion magazine because my style would have evaporated. That rule is just baloney. Another rule that seemed to be being defied by many women today is that at a certain age, I should not date men younger than me. Thanks to Demi Moore, that rule really does not apply anymore. However, I believe it might help if I actually looked like Demi when I proceeded to try to break this rule. Although these rules are not written down in any book, most females around the world know and live their lives by them.

One night I was sitting in a bar and looking at a very attractive man sitting at the other end. He smiled back at me and I thought, "Eureka!" I have discovered bar room gold. Then to my chagrin but not my dismay, a very swanky young blonde-haired woman came out from the restroom and proceeded to drape herself all over this guy. He was cute, looked like he was smart, and so why would I ever think he would be single? I cried all the way home because I wondered what this single life had in store for me. If I had to have any more nights of hanging out in bars with my friends while we all tried to look interested in the lame lines that were being tossed at us, I think I might opt for a nunnery. I had to fight awful hard to stay positive about this singles' experience, because that was the only way that I was going survive. I made it home that night to a still and lonely house. The positive meter was dipping. I made it to my bed and tried not to feel the empty space that was next to me. I plumped up the pillows to help me feel some warmth lying next to me. With the comfort of the pillows surrounding me, I made it through another night without waking every hour. While my options for romance looked dim, I knew that I could make it to the next day. Though many such days loomed ahead blaring at every opportunity that I was now alone, I was going to take it as a call to arms. My revelation was that just finding a man was not the answer. I had to learn how to be okay falling asleep alone. I needed to remember that just having a body next to me was not always a comfort, as my marriage would attest to.

I called my friends and they suggested that maybe meeting for coffee might be a better idea than alcohol at seven in the morning.

My friends talked me down from the ledge of unreason and buoyed my spirit while agreeing with my new battle plan. It was not the first time they would have to do this, and it would not be the last. I learned firsthand that going through life changes can make or break a friendship. The divorce put a completely new spin on the hurtles my friendships would have to overcome. As I mentioned before, some married friends saw me as a predator just waiting to pounce on their unsuspecting husbands. When that happened, I knew they would not be my friends for long and most likely never were. Then there were my friends that loved me for me. Those friends told me all the time how proud of they were of me. Those friends sent me cards to help lift my spirits. They told me that I was amazing and beautiful, and that they believed that I would be happily married in a short amount of time. Those friends took time out of their very busy days to listen to me when I felt small and sad. They were loving and compassionate, and never made me feel that I was driving them crazy with my incoherent singles babbling. They were precious, wonderful gifts and I would never forget the love and support they gave me. My friends became more than just friends; they became my family.

By looking to one day at a time, I knew I could do this. I would not settle for just anything. I wanted "IT," and I was willing to wait for as long as he took to find me. I was willing to enlist plenty of activities such as crochet, knitting, latch hook rugging, or even quilting to keep myself busy so I would not be thinking too much. I had plenty of material at my disposal to read; magazines, books, pamphlets and even cereal boxes could keep me enthralled for a moment. The first task I decided to undertake was to organize every room in my house, starting with the closet.

The closet in my bedroom was a stepping-stone for me. The closet held not only my clothes, but also the LCS's clothes. There was more than just cotton, wool and synthetic fabrics hanging there waiting for me to browse through. The closet was the keeper of memories. There were bills that we had paid during our marriage, suitcases we took trips with, letters and cards that we had sent to one another, and clothes I had bought him for his birthday that he never wore. The years of our marriage were safely tucked away with mothballs protecting it all; but no matter how much cedar lining we put down, the closet and its contents had become moth eaten. There was no way to patch up the dreams and hopes that were gone. When the LCS first left, I tried not to look at his side of the closet. Yet, no matter how hard I tried to ignore the shirts, pants and jackets hanging there, they kept inserting their way into my view. That was something that I could not have anymore. I purchased copious amounts of plastic bags, called the charities, and started filling. Going, going, gone were all the parts of him that he had left behind. When I finished with the job, all the memories and pain sat on the floor waiting to be taken away. My clothes were happy to be able to stretch out and get comfortable on the opposite side of the closet.

These little pieces of the recovery puzzle were essential to me becoming a new and whole person. I changed the side of the bed that I slept on because I used to let him sleep by the door so that he could protect me from whatever went bump in the night. Now I slept on his side because I was going to be my own protector. I began not to feel so lonely climbing into my bed at night and enjoyed the fact that I could read, watch TV, sing opera songs, and would never hear someone telling me stop because, "I'm trying to sleep" I could have two blankets on the bed and be cuddly and warm instead of hearing, "It's so hot in here," as the blankets were whipped off the bed. I put as many throw pillows on the bed as I wanted, and there was no one to complain that they were a pain in the butt. I snored, ate crackers in bed, and watched all the romance riddled movies I wanted without disturbing anyone. Freedom was enjoyable in the bedroom. Nevertheless, at some point, it was apparent that it had been some time since I actually had been "free" in my bedroom.

Should I say sex?

When I was married, sex became something that was just another part of my week, month, or in some cases, year. It was not something that I obsessed about, it was just the icing on the cake of my life. I had good sex in an okay marriage, and I was one of the lucky ones. If I had loved and desired my partner with a passion that surpassed most other people's understanding, then I would have been an anomaly. In my marriage, sex had turned into the Saturday night performance of a one-time show with a 9:30 - 9:45 curtain.

There are different phases to the sexual world as married people. In the beginning, I experienced the honeymoon sex that occurred from the first night of my honeymoon. When I say the first night of my honeymoon, I do not mean the night after the wedding, when we returned to our overpriced hotel room before departing to our chosen exotic location. The real honeymoon sex started the night we actually arrived in our exotic location and imbibed too many mai tai's at the poolside bar. As a newly married couple, my spouse and I, discovered that the first night we were married, we were not going have sex. Why? Because we were too overwhelmed and exhausted. I had spent ten hours soaking up every event of the biggest day of my life. I had only ingested champagne and one chicken skewer, so the last thing I wanted was sex. The first thing we wanted upon our arrival at the hotel was food. Then I wanted sleep and I wanted it bad. The myth of passionate, romantic, rose-petal sex had been crushed, and my spouse and I curled up with the food basket from the caterer and the remote control. After eating like a dog on amphetamines, I slumped over into the brie en croute and fell asleep. The next morning, I awoke to find a large slice of brie attached to my cheek and my newly acquired mate snoring loudly beside me. In my head, I shrieked as I became conscious to the fact that I had just glimpsed my future. This is what marriage was really like. This was how I would spend countless nights, hopefully not falling asleep in the brie, but definitely falling asleep to late night television and my snoring mate.

The first morning of our life together, I woke up my husband by shouting in his ear. He threw a cheese puff at the wall as he awoke with a start. He glanced at me as I was scraping the last of the brie off my cheek. We then began the psychotic and typical rush to get ready for the insanely early departure time I had set. When planning the honeymoon, I thought that an early departure would allow optimum honeymoon time. I did not factor in the hangover from brie and wedding cake. This rushing around was a ploy as well. If we rushed around, then neither of us would have to face the fact that our dismal attempt at a romantic first night had been precedented by food and television. Oh, how the mighty have fallen. This revelation would stay unsaid in both our subconscious. It would rear its ugly head at some point I was sure. After we raced and dashed to the airport, I discovered that I had forgotten something. I did not forget my curling iron. I did not forget the shoes that matched my dress I planned to wear at dinner. I forgot the one item that my husband would actually miss catching a plane for. I forgot my birth control pills! The all-important and absolutely necessary pills that my husband was ready to book another flight for so we could drive home to retrieve them. We only had one, okay maybe two, items on the agenda for our honeymoon. One was to have enormous amounts of sex. The other was to follow that up with copious amounts of alcohol. A line item on the agenda was *not* to make a baby. We were lucky because our best man was staying at our house, and he volunteered to bring these important pharmaceuticals to us. He did this incredible deed of driving through a wicked hangover, because his ex-wife had forgotten her birth control pills on their honeymoon, and nine months later, they had their daughter.

The honeymoon was wonderful. Well, we were in a tropical locale where balmy breezes created a cocoon of good feelings, and so did the piña coladas. We basked in the love, attention, and romance of newly married individuals. Once we returned home, we began the transition from being dating partners to husband and wife. The sex was still new, wonderful, and often. We did not have anyone to worry about except each other. There was a freeness and lack of responsibility that created a cocoon around us. We loved freely and with our whole hearts. We were still dating each other even though we were married. We spent time worrying about the other person's needs primarily. There were adjustments to be made as I learned to live with another person and deal with the little idiosyncrasies that I did not know or care had existed before because I loved him. Everything was going along smoothly and our responsibilities were few. After a couple of years of this bliss, we made the choice to begin to procreate and with this decision, we moved into the second part of life as a married couple.

Deciding to have a baby brought a new dimension to our bedroom. It was no longer just the place where we would rest and commingle, it became the room where we would make our child. Once the decision to have a baby was made and we were both onboard with the idea, the real changes began. There are two trains of thought on the idea of conceiving. One is to have sex as much and as often as possible. Then there is the more scientific plan of sex at just the right moment and time. Either way the sex has begun its metamorphosis. Spontaneity seemed a thing of the past, as my spouse and I tried for the new addition to our family.

After much deliberation with the actual act, I was pregnant. My body, hormones, and desires started to change almost immediately. After a few months of pregnancy, my hormones started kicking in and suddenly I became a completely different creature. I thought about sex all the time. My spouse found himself saying, "Not tonight honey, I have a headache." Then the day came when I felt the baby move for the first time. With this stupendous and phenomenal experience, I became a mother. In pregnancy, change is the mantra. Each moment my attitudes would change. Once I felt the baby kick, sex was something I could care less about. Changes happened in strange ways. I had never been a huge eater, but now I could put away a ten-pound steak in about three seconds flat. This aspect did not amuse my spouse. In fact, there would be times when I would catch him looking at me as if he did not know who I was.

Another change that greatly impeded our sex life was sleep. When I was pregnant, all I thought about was when I could go to sleep. I would wake up and wonder when I could take a nap. I could fall asleep standing in line for the groceries. I could fall asleep while washing my hair in the shower. I could fall asleep at the dinner table. I could certainly fall asleep as soon as my rear end hit any soft surface. Being as before the pregnancy I did not need much sleep, this aspect was causing great concern. The bigger joke was as the pregnancy progressed and I got bigger and bigger, I strongly became reacquainted with my previous obsession with having sex. This both attracted and repelled my spouse. On one hand, he was interested in sex, but his child was growing in there. He believed that when we had sex, our child would have a front row seat. He even said once, "Won't I hurt his head?" We are talking confident here! I did not care what his reservations were, because I wanted sex and I wanted it now. I would do whatever it took to get it, and I did.

Then the baby was born. Nothing will kill romance, spontaneity, or sex faster than an eight-pound baby will. Suddenly there was nothing as important to me as cleaning, cuddling, feeding, washing, and staring at the new bundle of joy in our home. Sleep became something that I would snatch in bittersweet moments. Together my husband and I realized that sleep was more precious than sex. I would rather have five uninterrupted hours of sleep than taking part in the best, dirtiest, all encompassing sex I had ever had. This shift of priorities, no matter how subtle they might have been, created the new basis of our sex life. Sex became more of a type of snatching affair…before the kids woke up…before the kids came home…before the kids come down in the middle of the night. Sex became a timed event that must be done quickly and thoroughly. I called it stealth sex. We did not have those long, languorous sexual encounters anymore. When we were lucky enough to engage in the event, we were up against the closet wall while our child was watching a movie in the family room. We got good at timing everything so that we could fit both of our needs into the time it takes a kid to finish breakfast. The race was on. Can I have an orgasm before the next commercial?

As the years progressed and another kid was added to our mix, there came more responsibilities that summarily killed the stealth sex. Our relationship was older, my husband was older, and the kids were older which caused new and some-time insurmountable obstacles. On a night when the passion might be percolating, a child asking to come into our bed definitely killed the moment. Our irresponsible sex made way for the predictable Saturday night sex of the old married couple. As sleep had become an even higher priority for my spouse, it would oftentimes be the deciding factor in whether or not I would get sex. Would he rather have an orgasm, or would he rather sleep? The balances were teetering often to the side of sleep. I felt that sex could not get more boring; and while I knew that most of my friends' lives were in the same pattern, it still did not stop me from speculating that there should be more.

In a group of women talking about sex; because let's admit it ladies, it is a high priority conversation, there seems to be two types of women. There are the individuals that let it all hang out telling you more than you really wanted to know, and those that do not tell you anything. Of course alcohol can often loosen up the tongues of the tight-lipped; but then you probably wished that they had never spoken, because invariably these were the women who were getting sex and often. When the question was asked, "How often do you have sex?" Most women said twice a month, once a week, maybe even every two months; but rarely did I hear every other day. When this statement was uttered, drinks were lifted and then refilled to a chorus of, "Oh my god." After being privy to many of these conversations, I can safely say that few people are actually satisfied with the amount of sex they are having. The individuals that are not getting it at all are, of course, completely frustrated. Oddly enough, the individuals that are getting too much are also completely frustrated. So what is a girl to do?

The variety in the sexual lives of people is extensive. With my divorce, the idea of sex was worrisome. It had been years since I had been with anyone but my husband. What if I could not pass muster in the world of the thirty-something divorced dating world. While I had interesting obstacles in the single world, the same sorts of confusions were occurring in my friends' married world. I heard of couples that went on a sex hiatus. These couples are married and happily so, but both partners have decided that sex was too much work and they would get back to it once they have a little more time. There are those unbelievable couples that still do it every other day, and they are a topic of serious contemplation. The world of grown-ups seemed to have many aspects of youth. I felt like when I was a teenager and all I did was think about sex or about how much my boyfriend in high school wanted sex. I remembered those days of wondering if I should "do it" or not. I reverted to that obsessive fascination about sex and relationships and knew that it was time to start doing something about it.

I should delve deeper into the sub-category that I found myself falling into after the LCS's departure, the newly separated and moving towards a divorce category. Now where do you suppose I was going to find a man that wanted to date a woman with two kids, a dog, and an ex-husband? You know how they have biker bars, gay bars and such, but did they have a recently separated and scared to have sex bar? Was there a location where a woman with a few stretch marks was considered the hottest thing ever? If so, would someone call me with the directions?

Once again, I was sent to the singles bars. What I found waiting for me were the same guys that had been shopping around with lines like, "Do you come here often," twenty years ago. They were still dropping these lines, only now they were twenty years older with a little more around the their middles and a little less on the top of their heads. After my first encounter at such a place, I briefly thought – maybe the LCS was not so bad. I mean, what was a little lying and cheating among friends. It was a dismal picture in the world that I was about to become a qualified member of, and more than that, it was very frightening. In the meantime, all I could think about after several months in forced celibacy was, "I NEED sex."

My enlightened friends told me it was time for a field trip. We were going to a sex shop. These stores have kept up with the times and are not filled with scary sex objects. They are user-friendly stores that cater to the women of today and what they want. The stores were pretty and mostly pink and one even had potpourri out in the bathroom, at least I think it was potpourri. Truth was I did not even have to go to the store if I did not want to. I could shop online and have everything delivered right to my door in a plain brown box with no return address so that no one would be able to tell what was inside. That was if I did not have parental security on my computer.

However, what I needed, they did not sell at any store. While all women need love and attention, a woman going through a divorce needs all this with reassurance thrown in. I needed to feel that I was still desirable. I wished that there was a store, country, or far-off jungle, where I could buy this reassurance. Then I could mix it up, drink it in a tea, and put it to use. The sexual aspect was important and necessary of course, but what was essential was the touch of someone's hand filled with love. That is what makes sex what it is, for most women. Women like sex and some women even *love* sex, I mean, I have seen cable. Yet, what most women are searching for in the act of sex, is something completely different from what men are looking for. For men it appears to be mostly physical. For women it seems mostly emotional. As usual with men and women, we are at two polar opposites.

Having dinner out one evening my friend uttered, "You know marriage is a completely unnatural act." Looking at her as if she had just uttered that the sky was going to fall, I asked her to elaborate. She continued to say that to take two strangers and make them live together while loving only one another for eternity, was not something natural that people are able to do. Wondering about this concept, it made some sense to me. I thought back to my own courtship with the LCS and how most everything we did ended up in sex. We would go out to dinner and then have sex. We would go to see a play and then have sex. We would...well you get the picture. In essence, the only reason that any man or woman ever really appeared to get together in the first place, was that the pheromones were flowing so strong. I had overlooked all the things that were probably going to drive me mad in the future with the LCS, because the sex was good. By the time I realized that these quirks really bugged me and were quite possibly going to affect my sanity, I was hooked into several years of marriage. Start over? I think not. I weighed the annoyance factor and figured that I could still love him even with his faults, because he loved and desired me with all my quirks. That is what makes marriage work, at least most of the time.

CHAPTER SEVEN

Is this an epidemic?

s I tried on some strappy silver sandals, a woman sitting next to me told me they were cute and I had to get them. I told her thanks and being the excellent communicator that I am, I told her how I was getting divorced. "So am I," she said.

I could not believe it, another one. I told her how the singles organization I joined was having a disco bus around the city and I had signed up to get down, and boogie, oogie, oogie, with some friends. I told her that I believed getting a divorce was an epidemic. She agreed and we followed up with some practical information where she could sign up for the same singles organization. I think I might need to start getting a commission from them, because I was a walking billboard as to their merits of bringing us divorcees up to speed in the world of singles. After I left the store, carrying the silver sandals and a cute pair of boots that were half-off, I could not stop thinking about this woman.

Every day I would meet a woman who was either going through a divorce or had just finished signing divorce papers. These women I have met were not ogres. They did not have horns growing out of their heads. They were smart, beautiful, and wonderful women who actually seem a bit awestruck at the marital predicament that they find themselves in. So what was going on in a vast number of men's heads that makes them leave these beautiful and desirable women to go out in search of what…the Holy Grail? I remember asking the LCS why he felt like he had to leave. He told me that he felt he had not accomplished anything with his life. He wanted to do exciting things, see the world, bungee jump, and maybe even skydive. I remarked to him that I would be willing to do most of those things with him, so why did he feel that he had to be alone to be able to enjoy these activities?

My belief is that men's brains short circuit at certain ages. It can vary as to what age it will manifest. Some men are in their thirties. Some men are in their forties. It can even happen to men in their fifties and sixties. When the synapses start misfiring, they can no longer see the beauty of their wife and home. All they can see is chains on the doors and bars on the windows. They believe they must make a last ditch attempt to go out and become a lead singer in a rock band, even if they cannot really sing. These men feel that if they do not get out and get out quick, they will die rotting, never to have lived a life of bliss and excitement. If they cannot leave outright because propriety prevents them, then they will find other means of escape. I think we all know what I mean here – the other woman.

The other woman can fall into several categories. She can be the woman who knows the man she is seeing is married and she just does not care. There is the other woman who knows the man she is seeing is married, but is sure that she can wrest him out of the little woman's grip. There is the other woman who has no intention of ending up with this man but certainly is making this mid-life crisis work to her advantage. Whatever category she falls into, the other woman will be despised and reviled by decent women everywhere. However, before we fire up the stoning machine and get ready to rumble, we women need to remember that the one perpetrating the crime is the man. The LCS had made a decision that for whatever reason his life was humdrum and dull and he needed a bit of drama to spice it up.

I remember asking the LCS why he could not have just gone out and bought a sports car, and at least I could have benefited from this mid-life crisis too? I was saying or rather screaming the fact that he could have found a less damaging way of facing his mortality, especially a way that would not have taken me down with him. Yet, being a subscriber of the theory that everything happens for a reason, I had to believe that this complete upheaval of my life was happening for some greater good, and I needed to be patient to await the outcome.

Back to the silver sandals mentioned previously. Signing up for an exciting night out in the city with three of my friends was a way to make the weekend a bit more glamorous. The singles organization was sponsoring a bus trip of all the hot dance spots in our city. My friends and I thought that riding a "party" bus around for the night to enjoy the nightspots without any worry about driving while intoxicated sounded fun. We got ready to have an exciting night filled with dancing, drinking, and of course, hopes of finding a special someone. We met at my house for a pre-party and the laughs were flowing. Being that we were of the same age category, we were enjoying reminiscing about our high school days. Honestly, our preparation felt a bit high schoolish as we listened to the music of our glory days. We were filled with anticipation and expectation. Stress on the word "expectation."

This word is a dirty word in my book. The word, expectation has destroyed many a love, life, and relationship. Expectations are what caused my outlook to be clouded by what I wanted and needed. I would watch movies, read books and listen to others who set my expectations high, high, and even higher. I could say, "Oh I have no expectations about that." However, that was an out and out, bold-faced lie. I had huge expectations about most things in life that I experienced. I went into every situation expecting something, whether it be a good drink or meeting the love of my life. There was no immunity from expectations.

Back to the subject at hand, the wearing of the slinky and intriguing silver shoes. Wearing those shoes made me feel like Dorothy in the Land of Oz. As I buckled the strap, I felt that these shoes would bring me magical powers. In these shoes, I would transcend myself and become the billboard image of myself that I had in my head. As my friends and I drove towards our location, all of us had some form of this transcendence occur. We were no longer divorced, near forty-year-olds; we were hot mommas of the night. We were twenty-five, clear skinned, lanky, tanned and desirable. As we arrived at the first disco, we were dressed to kill and ready to pounce. In we walked to the designated location, and all of us felt the feeling of unbelief wash over us. Once again, the dirty expectations had reared their heads and we were not prepared for what awaited us.

The group was nice, clean and very kind, I am sure. However, there was no man of my dreams sitting on a barstool. There was no soul mate ordering a drink. There were just people like me - people who looked at me with their own expectations. My friends and I decided that we must help quiet our expectations by having drinks, and lots of them.

After a couple of cocktails, we were approached by the leader for the evening. As she approached, that billboard in our mind was put to the test. Standing in front of us, was this bouncy twenty-year-old that obviously had no trouble in the singles market. She was condescendingly informing us that we had to wear an obnoxious wristband that made me reminisce of the water slide park I visited in the summer with my kids. Crashing sounds in our brains sounded as we were faced with our blaring reality. We were about to don these ridiculous wristbands and be driven around the city to go bar hopping. I wondered about the necessity of wristbands as I was a forty year-old woman; am I going to forget which bus I am on only to be saved from misdirection because I am wearing a wristband. To add further insult to injury, the wristband could not have been unobtrusive to disappear into my flesh; no, it was a red, white and blue flag wristband that screamed, "Look at me!" or at the very least inspired people to want to break out into the national anthem! As we rambled out to the bus the adventure began. My friends and I were now realizing how incredibly stupid we looked as forty-year-old mothers emerging from a party bus to enjoy a cruise around a bar. Even fortified with alcohol, we realized that we could not start a conversation with anyone that we potentially might want to date because we would have to cut it short by saying, "I'm sorry, I'd love to stay and chat, but my party bus is leaving." That sentence would be the kiss of death to any potential suitor.

However, we endeavored to make our own fun so while the rest of the bus was rather staid and quiet, our foursome decided to make the back of the bus the cool zone. We were dancing and singing and having quite a fun time. The rest of the bus was looking at us and wondering a couple of things: how much alcohol did we drink and how could they make their way back towards our seats. I must admit that we were making the best of the situation in regard to our expectation marker. We all felt that since our future love was not present on the party bus, being together we could make our own fun. This charade seemed to work until the next club. Then the realization of my expectations hit me like a brain freeze from a frosty margarita .

The club was conveniently and picturesquely located across from a cement-making factory. It was small, dark and hot. These are the three essential ingredients for most successful dance clubs. The party bus deposited us in front of the club and we made our way straight to the front of the line. Once inside, the techno beat started throbbing in my ears. For the entire hour and a half that we were there the same song played, at least it sounded like the same song. Looking around the club, I was struck with the age ratio and how it related to me - it didn't. I was old. In fact, I could have been a mother to most of these club goers. Heated up with the party bus experience, I started dancing. I became oblivious to the amount of people in the room. When I came up from my dance-induced euphoria, I saw that I was one in a crowd of about sixty people that were sharing the same very miniscule dance floor. Everyone was sweating and gyrating and I thought, "Where the hell am I?" It was somewhere between sighting the Paris Hilton look-alikes looking at me and having two girls trying to funk dance me while yelling, "Go mamma!" that I realized who, where, and what age I was. I went to the bathroom and a neon sign went off above my head. "You are old!" it flashed.

I realized what I must have looked like to the younger members of this crowd. When the youthful spirit of my twenties had been channeling my body, I saw a couple of kids look at me and duck into the bathroom. I am sure the conversation in the facilities went something like, "Dude, was that my mother?" After facing the realism staring back at me in the bathroom mirror, I went to see how my friends were accepting this awful but stark truth. I understood then that not everyone had the same expectation factor I did. In fact, one friend was freak dancing with a very young and buff dance suitor, while my other friend was just plain freaking! The last member of our posse, or should I say passé, was resting quietly by the fire. Yes, I said fire. The one accoutrement you do not expect to see in a dance club filled with five hundred or so gyrating people, is a fire pit. As the fire blazed, I knew that my friends and I were enjoying our own versions of reality that night.

Some of us were choosing to escape from the harshness of being too old. Others, like myself, knew that no amount of dancing would make this ridiculous dance club the right place to be. I was too old for this place, these people, and this music. I was enjoying the idea of the ride. However, in my case the ride had already left without me. No matter how much I danced or drank, the expectations I set were dashed in the first five minutes after we arrived. What I wanted, and I would not even admit to myself that I was looking for, was not there. Him. The One. The person we were all searching for. Our prince, our soul mate, our dream was not there in that group, and he definitely was not going to be found on the age-defying dance floor. No, it would be one more night that my heart would find that elusive love lacking, one more night that my expectations would go to bed alone. It would be another night where I would go home and think, "What am I doing with my life?"

This pondering of my life choices was happening over and over as I went through this divorce. There were so many levels of what I was experiencing. I was daunted by the amount of women going through this process. On any given day, I could find a woman that has just been left, followed by a woman that was in the throes of being left, being shadowed by a woman that was starting to come out of being left and dating. Like grief, divorce has a process. It actually feels more like circles of hell, but it is a process and I began on the same dazed level as other women before me. I stepped into the "get me alcohol quick" level. Then I proceeded to an "I don't need a man" level, followed by the "I am a loser who will be living alone with many cats" level. I could not rush any of these processes. I had to feel each level and let time work and heal me. I doubted myself. I doubted if I could succeed to become a new and improved person. I used to look at myself and wonder if I would make it, but I *was* making it. Everyday and every moment that I continued on this uncharted life plan was success. I could not wrap my brain around the idea of dating again, but my heart wanted to run right out and find someone to replace the one I lost. My mind knew that I was not ready for that. I was not ready to start all over with someone new when I had not even finished with the last relationship. Yet in this society where being alone is worse than the plague, I found that there is a time and place for loneliness. In fact, loneliness was part of the healing. Once I realized that I actually wanted to be alone, I knew I was healing. I felt a bit as if I should be wearing ruby slippers and have a scarecrow attached to my arm. The process was in full swing, and I was determined to heal completely and be ready for the next stage in my life.

CHAPTER EIGHT

Now we wait!

Waiting was a very hard thing to do as patience was a rare commodity in my life. Waiting meant that I must sit back and let life follow its course. I must endure the day-to-day. I must learn to let life be what it was to be. Sounds like a saying from a fortune cookie I know, but it was more than that. Patience is something that many people lack today. I am one of those people. It is not surprising that I am that way since I exist in a world where commercials are only fifteen seconds long and waiting more than three minutes for food was not acceptable. Our society, and I as a member, had decided that patience was something we could live without. Why wait for the great experiences of life to make their way to me when I could go out and try to direct them into my life's flight plan? And while it was so great to be motivated, there was a fine line between being proactive and trying to control every event in my life. Control can be a tricky stumbling block. Since my life was like a puzzle, I knew that chance, luck, and fate had a large part to where my path lead. It did not help that from child-hood I was led to believe that someday, if I waited long enough, my Prince Charming would come to rescue me from the boring day-to-day life in which I existed. He would whisk me off to the imaginary castle where birds sang all the time; and each time I went shopping, the clothes would all be fifty percent off. I felt I had to be rescued from reality by the prince; however, those fairytales always ended with the rescue and never come back for a follow-up several months later. If I revisited the situation five months later, I believe the Prince's crown would be a bit askew and the Princess's gown would be stained, for there is no such thing as a fairytale. I thought that my Italian man was going to be my fairytale; but alas, he ended up only being a tale. A wise friend said to me in one of our Grey Goose sessions, "If you can laugh about it in three years, then have a drink; if you can't, then have a cry." I wonder if Snow White lived by this credo?

Here I was waiting. What was I waiting for? Everything, I believed. Even when the LCS left and I was alone, which was my worst fear come to life, I learned that I was okay today. I would be okay tomorrow. The fear I had my whole life was not unbearable. I did not shrivel up and die being alone; to the contrary, I grew until I found the strength to see this as my second chance at life. Time was going to march on and it did. All I had to learn to do was to wait with patience and openness to what the universe had in store for me. I needed to recreate my fairytale so I waited, and waited, and waited, and waited. Some days it was easy to get up and go about my life with a smile on my face and joy in my heart. Other days, it was hard just to pull the covers off my face. The days that were challenging were the stepping-stones that led me down to the path of recovery. Every day that I felt I had made it across one of those stepping-stones was a good day. The days I slipped off, were the hard days. On those hard days, I had to find a way to combat the angst that lived in my heart.

I found that shopping for a new shirt could make the day and a moment pass a bit brighter. Eventually though I realized that all the shirts in the world were not going to take the place of love in my heart; but it did not hurt to look good while I was waiting. I remembered how when I was a little kid, waiting for things seemed to take forever. Being a child meant thinking that summer lasted forever. Those three months pardoned from school was an endless supply of laughter, fun, sleepovers, warm nights riding my bike, happiness, and the sweet innocence of youth. I could wait for anything, because I did not know what I was waiting for. When I grew up, the harsh reality of knowing what I was waiting for was what caused me to be unable to contain the impatience in myself. I knew that I was waiting for that special person that was going to make me laugh, glow, and feel whole. I knew that I was ready to learn the attributes in myself that would lead me to my future goals. Because I knew what I was waiting for, I had the hardest time being tolerant of the passing time. I decided I should go out and try to hurry my dream along against my better judgment. I was going to try to control the situation – bad choice. In trying to control anything that big, I would invariably end up waiting that much longer. A simple analogy kept running through my mind. Whenever I called a company and they put me on hold, I would listen to the tuneless, hold music for only so long before I finally became impatient and hung up the phone. My thinking was that if I called back maybe I could increase my odds of talking to someone sooner. Calling the number once more, I would simply be put on hold again, which created more wait time for me. In truth, I only pushed myself down on the list of non-patience mongers. Waiting cannot be rushed. Waiting is what it is, patience left on hold.

I decided I would become optimistic. Perhaps I had better prepare myself for that certain eventuality of being in a relationship. To do that I had to join the age of protection and go down and get myself some condoms. Ever the glass-half-full kind of girl, I knew I was going to need these important items at some time, hopefully in the near future; and I did not want to be caught without them. I enlisted the aid of a friend to go with me so that I was not alone perusing the condom aisle. My friend applauded my foresightedness and agreed that I would need protection and she was willing to accompany me for moral support.

There are two kinds of women in this world: those whose mothers told them about sex honestly informing them of contraception and its uses and those whose mothers pretended that sex did not exist, at least for their children. My mother happened to be the second type of mother. I remember once in college, my mother and I went to lunch where I broached the subject of sex with her. She all but put her hands up to her ears and sang, "la, la, la, la," so she would not have to hear my words. Needless to say, I was not well versed in the contraception issue.

Returning to the condom aisle, I stood there with my friend looking at the various types and brands of condoms and was flabbergasted. There were over twenty different types of condoms. There were condoms for his pleasure, is that not just being redundant? There were condoms for her pleasure, which of course I felt I should buy, but then felt that it might be a tad selfish. There were king-sized condoms, which was very optimistic. There were lightly lubricated, heavily lubricated, not lubricated at all, condoms that you cannot feel, ones that have ribs, and ones that are different colors. I looked at my friend and said, "Which one?"

She looked back at me and replied, "I have no idea."

There we were debating the benefits and drawbacks of each type while it seemed every single person that came to shop in the store that day passed down our aisle. We both kept our heads down in fear that our child's teacher, principal, or soccer coach was going to come strolling down the aisle and see us standing front and center in the prophylactics section. We broke out into so many fake conversations that I actually became confused as to why I was there. Finally, the coast was clear and I reached up and grabbed a middle-of-the-road-hope-to-pleasure-all brand. It was time for the check out stand.

As I stood in line with my purchases, my friend abandoned me because the stress was starting to get to her. I just hoped that there would not be the price check nightmare. You know the one you always see on television, where the person is standing at the check-out line and the checker calls over the loud speaker for a price check on the rather embarrassing item you are purchasing. This being the day of scan codes, I could not see how I would have to endure such a predicament. I stood there waiting; having chosen a woman checker who I believed would be in silent sisterhood with me for my foresightedness. I became conscious that someone was calling my name behind me. I turned slowly, and there was a mother of one of my children's friends. Sitting right in front of her on the belt was "the condom you won't know even exists!" I quickly stepped in front of her to block her view of my indelicate item. I flicked my hand and perfectly timed the condoms to slip under the fishy cracker box. I used considerable stealth in keeping the embarrassing moment at bay. This was not going to be my world's most embarrassing moment. I was spared the humility. I breathed a sigh of relief and walked lightly out the door, safe in the knowledge that I was prepared when one day a man decided that he wanted to have carnal knowledge of my body.

Suddenly the night arrived. I went out with a friend for a drink. We were having a great time laughing and not worrying about anyone else in the bar, when he sat down and started talking to me. He was funny and sarcastic, and I found myself laughing at his jokes while flirting with him. We talked for a while and then he just got up and left. On most occasions that would have made me mad, but for some reason I really did not care. Hard to believe, but true. After all this time I had thought I wanted someone, I become conscious of the fact that I was having a wonderful time just being alone with my friend. I was just enjoying myself and not caring who or what might be out there. I continued my evening; and when leaving I walked out through the back exit. There he was. He was just sitting there talking to someone. I found myself joking with him that I did not liked being stood up, especially when I was sitting down. He laughed and I believe a flicker of fear crossed his face as he thought I was upset. I laughed and continued to give him a hard time. Eventually, he warmed up to the idea that I was just kidding and it was okay to tease back. That was when the tide turned.

He suddenly told me that he was going to kiss me. My answer straight away was, "Bullshit!" He grabbed me and kissed me. It was a warm and demanding kiss, and I was completely inspired to kiss him back the same way. In that kiss were nights of tears. In that kiss were frustrations and pains. In that kiss were longing and wants. I was allowing all of those emotions to be free and relishing this moment. I was not holding everything back to create an impossible relationship. I was not slamming the door on what could be. I was not telling myself that this was not right. I was going right down that irresponsible path and loving every minute of it.

After kissing like teenagers in my car for about a half-an-hour, my lips could not take anymore. I must admit freely that I said those cliché words, "Do you want to come back to my place?" (Oh my god, I was channeling Diane Keaton in *Looking for Mr. Goodbar*.) At that point, I was not thinking safety. I was letting my intuition and probably stupidity get the best of me. I needed this, I wanted it, and I deserved it. Oh, let's be honest, I wasn't thinking at all. For this night I was just feeling and being. This was not going to be a long-term relationship. This was going to be just what it was, a one-night stand.

Suffice to say, the condoms were used and functioned properly. Sorry to say, the gentleman did not. It was a disap-pointing reintroduction to the art of bed sport. Where he excelled in foreplay, he absolutely failed at in the actual act. I think that maybe I may have been partly to blame. I was a bit bossy in the actual moment. Let's face it, I have had eleven years of consistency and a completely new formula really shook me up in many ways.

After he left, I did not feel sad, lonely, or guilty. I just fell asleep. However, when the next morning dawned, the cold feeling started to roll in. I realized that I was grieving a bit of the old me. This was the new me, the free me. I was allowed to have sex with anyone I wanted with the proper protection. There was no reason not to. So why did I feel bad? Was it guilt towards the LCS? Was it self-deprecation? The guilt and the low feelings stemmed from the acceptance that I was not a one-night-stand kind of girl. I had convinced myself that no feelings were a good thing. I thought I was in control. Maybe I was in control, but what I could not ignore, was the fact that this was not what my heart was looking for. I needed the emotions and feelings that went with lovely and passionate lovemaking. I was not the type of girl that could just hook up with someone and go about my business as if nothing had happened. Another lesson learned. It was necessary for me to understand that what I was looking for was not a quick fix. I was looking for a long and fulfilling answer. I understood that day that waiting was not so bad if I was waiting for the right thing. I could wait forever for the right person and the right relationship and I intended to.

Do you have the time?

After the first post marriage sexual encounter I survived, I began to ascertain things about myself. The one-night stand did not seem to be the way for me; however, I was eager to engage in this new single-woman sex if I could have a meaningful relationship attached to the act. These revelations were important because they would determine my dating pattern for the next several months, years, or decades.

Watching my newly single friends, I observed different behaviors in regards to the new single sex. Some women surmised that they needed sex and plenty of it and any man was the right man for them. They frequented bars, clubs, and hot nightspots looking for Mr. Right Now. They continued to engage in emotionally free sex, until the time came that either they got sick of the unemotional quotient or they ran out of men. I watched as some of these women decided that it was time to be done with this overindulgence and go on a sex diet. Their behavior changed and they began to pick at the sex buffet or go into complete fast mode. Either way with their appetites having been satiated, the woman could go back to a normal pattern of sexual indulgence. It appeared to me that this sexual smorgasbord was a way for these women to feel something again. It became clear that the short-lived high they were receiving from the adulation and attention, helped to calm the river of insecurity and fear that was raging through their souls. They believed that returning to this sexual buffet would bring them the emotional nourishment they needed. They did not realize that this overindulgence mostly just led to a need for bicarbonate and a large burp.

On the other side of the voracious sexual smorgasbord, was the woman who had slapped on a chastity belt and threw away the key. I saw women who were more afraid of the idea of having sex with someone they had not known for years, than walking into a den of very hungry lions. Many of these women simply shut down all social interaction. They became the self-cloistered nuns of their own divorced nunnery. I had friends that faded from view until the only relationship I had with them was with their answering machine. I would invite these women to go out to dinner or to a movie and they would have more excuses than an Enron executive why they could not venture out of their homes. After a while, I surmised that they would have to go through their penance before they would be ready to leave their self-imposed solitary confinement and be ready to enter the secular world of dating.

I experienced the one-night-stand phenomena and determined that this type of love-fest was not for me, so I decided to take a different approach to dating. I needed emotions that ran deeper than, "What's your sign?" I determined that I would hold off on the roll in the hay, until I had found someone worthy of rolling around with. I needed to feel love, or the beginning of it, before I wanted to give that intimate part of me away again. I had been monogamous for many years, and that type of relationship worked well for me. It could be challenging to find someone worthy of monogamy. Hurt and pain would occur as I deemed someone worthy of my sexual favors. It was easy to be played by unscrupulous suitors. Yet it was a chance I was willing to take. I needed the emotional connection to be able to create the smoldering passion in bed. I needed the fire to sizzle on an intellectual level before there could be any sparks in the bedroom. There was a process for me. I needed steps to be able to graduate from foreplay. The possible suitors appeared to be finely tuned machines able to go from kissing to sex in thirty seconds. My idea of sleeping with someone, took many rests in the dating pit stops. I could not come roaring into bed, because that was not what I required. The physical part was good, but having my emotional needs met was better.

The games were on and the dating war started. It was a whirlwind of dinners, drinks, and movies. There were blind dates, so-so dates, and dates that should have not been. I saw every conceivable type of man and many that I had never conceived of. I chatted at dinner, over coffee and often times at my car door. The dates were good, bad, and unfortunately ugly. Many times the date was in some way strange. There was the man who would not look up at me for our whole meal, the man that needed to sit in a particular corner of a restaurant at a certain table in a certain waitress section, and there was the man who divided our bill with the accuracy of the head of the IRS. There was the man who could not seem to stop looking at other women at other tables while I was sitting right across from him. The man who invited me to meet him for coffee and did not pay for mine, nor did he order any for himself. Then there was the man that wanted me to move into his house the following week and take care of his children promising to make it worth my while financially. Finally, there was the man that would not stop sending me emails, even though I had explained that a twenty-year age difference was a problem for me.

I suffered through all these dress rehearsals, waiting for the right one to come along. Then he did. I met Sam (well, let's just call him that) and he seemed strangely okay. I waited for the other shoe to drop. I looked behind the words he was saying. I analyzed everything. No matter how hard I looked, it all seemed to add up to perfection or at least something vaguely resembling that. He called and we talked with no lulls in the conversation. We talked about everything and he was witty in all the right places. I laughed at all of his jokes because they were funny. The chemistry appeared to be working between us, but I was fearful to get excited about the prospect because that was when the door always slammed shut.

I feigned disinterest to my friends, but they knew me better than that. They could tell I was interested, because I spent an inordinate amount of time talking about him. As they listened to his laundry list of attributes, they had to admit that it sounded promising. However, they reminded me that it was too soon to tell and be careful.

These were the words I heard most often, "Be careful." I wondered if people thought that the act of separation or divorce caused my brains to leave too. The part of me that dated in my twenties still lived dormant in my brain; and as the dating frenzy occurred, that dormant part woke up, yawned, and came alive. I was not without tools in the dating arena. I actually had more tools at my disposal because now I was not operating on naiveté. I did not believe the guy who told me I looked like a model. I knew I did not resemble a model in any way, except that we were both females. I was better equipped than people thought to be dating. In fact, I was better equipped than I thought to deal with dating.

I decided that Sam was engaging enough, and I allowed the shield to crack around my heart. The gap only occurred for a moment, lest someone actually touch the heart underneath it. We went out and I laughed at his truly wonderful stories. Sam was funny. He was smart. Sam was fetching. I found myself wanting a bit more. I wondered what it would be like to kiss him. Sam did not appear to be a weirdo, but the night was young. Yet I had to wonder, why was he single? Why hadn't someone snapped him up? What was wrong with him? Of course, I couldn't ask him those questions, at least not yet. I decided to bide my time.

The titillating phone conversations continued. The smart and quirky emails made me smile. I began to believe that there might be something here. The guy liked me; that was obvious. That was when my mind began to play games with me. I started to wonder when Sam was going to call, and started to analyze why when he did not. The games were afoot. I remembered those dating games that all people played. The games that I particularly hated because I wasn't very good at them. The "I won't call her for two days because I don't want to seem too anxious" game; the "I will act distant so he doesn't know that I like him" game. These were the dating rituals that happen between men and women and would make even an Olympic athlete exhausted. The problem was that everyone seemed to play them. In fact, if I was not physically conditioned to play these games, I was going to be lost forever in the dating arena. I have never been the type that could function within the unseen parameters of the "dating game." I realized that even at the age I found myself, I was going to have to start training. This inevitability was obvious when I efficiently set myself up. I had spent wonderful quality time with Sam and figured that we were ready to step up to an actual date on an actual weekend. I had already worked out the itinerary in my head. He would ask me out for Friday night, and we would be so blissfully happy together that we would end up going out Saturday night and that might just turn into Sunday morning. In my dream of our dating weekend, we would have eaten, gone to museums, shopped and had the most awesome, stupendous and mind-blowing sex ever. All this would happen with an appropriately romantic music track following us around. It would be dating bliss.

Sam did not ask me out. He did not even call. Okay, what was going on? We had been tearing up the phone lines; and then screech the brakes are on, and I did not even get an invitation for drinks. I was a bit dumbfounded. A friend said that when someone does not do what we expect of them (there is that dirty word again) we end up making it all about us. Well that is rich; I mean I am not *that* self-centered. Am I? Why the silence? Because we all are self-centered. I was the center of my universe. I am sure even Mother Teresa had days where she felt that she looked bad in her habit.

Why was I so self-centered? It stemmed from the fact that as a child, I started my days off with my mother doing everything for me. She fed, wiped, cuddled, stroked and loved me more than any creature. When I started growing up, the loving was still there but it had slowly moved farther away. I was expected to do more for myself. I was expected to move away. Why would I want to move away from that wonderful, unconditional love? As I matured and learned that the kind of love I experienced as a child cannot continue forever, I began to believe that maybe it was something that I had done as a child that caused the retraction of my parents. I could have been cuter. Maybe my baby thighs were too roly-poly. It was something I did, I was sure of it. That belief would follow me around like a shadow through the rest of my time on earth. Anytime someone did not like something that I made, wrote, created, or said I would blame myself.

Insecurity is a word that is bantered around a lot these days. It has many meanings. It can mean one who is not sure of their self worth. It can mean something that is not strong enough. When I looked around at our world, I saw people changing everything about themselves to fit in. I saw a show on television where this woman had made a whole life having cosmetic surgery to perfect herself. She had multiple surgeries. She had garnered sponsors for these surgeries. She wrote a book on the subject of how to procure more cosmetic surgery. She was evoking others to join her pseudo-cult by creating a website dedicated to her crazy occupation. She made a career out of her insecurity. I watched this woman with the fascination of a car wreck. She was pretty. However, her beauty ended at her subcutaneous level. She could not have surgery on the one part of her that really needed it, her self-esteem.

I considered the insane desire this cosmetic addict had for perfection. She made a comment that stood out above the rest for me. Observing an intelligent, but normal looking woman on television this surgery-doll said, "Now what man is going to love her?" I felt my heart freeze for a second. I thought that the ordinary woman on the television did not deserve that. Someone loved her; I was sure of that. I was sure that this ordinary woman who was just like me, was loved for who she was inside. That was a concept that was impossible for this poor unfortunate but beautiful woman to comprehend, that people love us for who we are not just what we look like. In fact, most individuals became better looking based on the inner quality of who they are.

At dinner one evening, I listened incredulously as Sam began a diatribe about fake breasts. A short comment would have been okay; but half an hour later, I began to feel that he might be obsessed with this subject. He was not saying that he preferred fake breasts. He was really just joking about the incredible size differential of some woman's chests. Yet while he was talking, I felt my self-esteem begin to shrink. I felt that this man, who seemed to enjoy my non-enhanced organic breasts as well as my company, was saying that he would rather be with a woman with large fake breasts. The anger rose inside. The more I listened to his words, the more I could feel the jealousy and envy beginning to work its way up into my throat. I had to end it now. I succinctly told him the boobie conversation was over; and for the record, women usually do not consider fake boobs a subject for lengthy debate. Sam meant nothing derogatory towards me, he was merely commenting on a very apparent social trend.

However, I did a very wrong thing. I took his comments personally. My own inner demons reared their ugly heads and I let my insecurity spew itself from my brain as I uttered, "I decided to be different than everyone else around here and go on my personality." What made me say that? He earned many points with me when he responded with a compliment, but the damage had been done. I succeeded in putting myself down in front of a man that I liked. If I did not see myself as special enough to take on a fake pair of breasts, why should he?

Years, and I mean years, of negative thinking had created a woman that was not sure of a single thing. I knew that I was strong. I knew that I was witty. I knew that I was fun. What I did not know, however, cancelled out the great stuff I did know. In the immortal words of the good-hearted prostitute in *Pretty*

Woman, "the bad stuff was easier to believe." That was true. I believed the bad about myself so quickly. The good had to be pushed on me, while I sat and denied that it was true. I created the insecurity in myself. I believed my own bad press.

I thought of a world where every woman believed herself lovely. A world where everyone was happy with who they were. This world, where any type of beauty was true, could exist as long as I believed in it. After watching that plastic surgery addict and feeling distraught at my own self-inflicted humiliation, I become conscious of something. I was going to change. The time had come to value myself. I was ready to utter my own battle cry. I was going to be proud of who I was just as I was. I was going to succeed. I was not going to sit around and wait for a man to call for a date ever again. I was going to live my life, not wait for some other person to validate my world. I was stepping out on the recovery road and adding another mile to my emotional pedometer. It was time to move on and begin my new life as my new self.

I realized that I needed help to keep this relationship on track. Being an emotional purist, I acted from the heart and sometimes I needed the head to balance out the feeling part. It became apparent that I needed a coach to help me understand the incredibly tricky mind of man. I had a girlfriend that had the uncanny knack of knowing how men thought, and I intended to use her knowledge. Women that can understand the mind of a man do exist. They are not urban legends. Luckily, one was my good friend. I called for help! She listened as I unloaded my dump truck of questions I intended to ask the man on our next date. She breathed out slowly, trying desperately not to slap me across the face, as I told her how I was going to get the answers that I needed. After my expulsion of future inquiries, she only uttered one word, "No." What was wrong with asking for my emotional needs to be met in this manner? Calmly she stated, "Do not put the cart before the horse."

These wise words emanated from a steady emotional brain. These statements were hard to comprehend since my emotional brain had recently undergone a total renovation. I was ready to sabotage something that could potentially head to greatness by violating this man's emotional airspace too soon. Of course, this behavior had its reasons for surviving. Its mission was to extract this individual from my life before he could hurt me. I knew he would hurt me, so why not make a preemptive strike. It was amazing how I was reenacting over and over the same scenario without even being aware that I was doing it. I was ready to assault this man over imaginary wrongs I felt were being done to me. Thank goodness for my friend's great advice. She told me to calm down. She calmly gave me a directive, "No matter what, you are not to call or email him. She stated the obvious to me, telling me to go make plans and live my life. Then she articulated those two words I barely could abide, "Just wait."

I followed her directions to the letter. I waited. I did not call or write. I made plans for myself to go out for dinner, movies, and drinks; and just when my dialing and typing finger started to get itchy, it happened! He called. Sam asked me out for that same night; and bravely, I told him I had other plans. I heard the disappointment in his voice. I was setting the tone now. I was quietly teaching him that I was not going to sit around and wait for him because I had a life that I was going to lead. I explained that my week was busy, and he seemed sad that I was not going to be available to spend time with him. It was wonderful. Instead, we made plans to see each other for coffee later that week. At our rendezvous later in the week, I was armed with my newly minted strong-girl shell. Sam and I enjoyed what turned out to be a three-hour walk filled with wonderful conversation.

I was beginning to like Sam. It seemed that both of us were working on our dating learning curve. I began to include this man into my world, which was the right way to shape a relationship. In the past, I had always given up everything for the man of my moment. If the current beau called, I made sure I was available. Actually, even if he did not call, I was available. Dating now was different. I had kids, work, dogs, chores, shopping, cleaning and a multitude of things that I had to accomplish. When I told someone I was busy, it was the absolute truth.

Ladies, if you have a pen close by, now is the time to get it out and underline the following passage: What women do not seem to understand about men is that men are hunters. For hunters, the thrill of anything they catch is the chase. Prey must be elusive for a man to be intrigued enough to track it into the bush. There are steps to enticing a man that I wanted to track me. If I trussed myself up and threw myself on their doorstep, then they would simply step over me to continue on their way. Men have been hunters since the beginning of time. This ability is innate in their genes; but with no more saber tooth cats to chase, women have become the chosen prey. If we women do not make it interesting and challenging, then the men simply are not going to pursue.

Consider the example of a woman who does not give a man who wants to date her the time of day. She will never return his phone calls and continuously turns him down for dates, and still the man is panting at her door to take her out. Why? Because her disinterest starts the competitive hunt gene to start firing to this man's brain. He must have this woman because she does not seem to want him. The hunt gene and the competitive gene go hand in hand, and these smart and elusive women know this. This is why more men seem to be interested in me when I am happily dating someone else. Women have a hard time with this concept, because the women I described above are usually given a name that rhymes with "itch." We are raised to be polite and considerate, so behavior such as not returning phone calls would be rude. That is our mistake. However, I only need to remind every woman, that all of us have fallen head over heels for the guy that did not pay *us* the time of day.

When I state that I do not want to play games, I do not mean that I am not interested in playing backgammon. It means that I do not want to play the subtle and not so subtle games that are entrenched in the dating world. When I dated, it felt as if someone entered me in the decathlon without giving me the rulebook. Nevertheless, being unavailable created a hum of interest in Sam. The hum was getting louder, and I think I may have effectively wrested the control away from his superior hunting fingers. Yet just as I stopped admiring myself for being so quick, he turned the games around to his favor.

Sam and I had plans for mid-week when he stopped communicating with me altogether. I started to panic. Being new to the rules for engagement, I decided I needed more stealthy advice. My friend was ready with more vital information. She told me to simply email him the day before our date and ask if everything was still on. I followed her instructions to the letter. Letting go of this angst was imperative. I needed to understand that if this relationship and this man were the right one for me then it would work out. We think that we are in control of everything that happens to us; however, there is so much at work that is not controlled by human hands. I decided that whoever was up there had a lot more understanding about what I needed than I ever could.

I lived my life; and in the interim, I forgot about the email I had sent, our impending date, and actually almost forgot about Sam. Then the phone rang. He called because he had responded to the email I had sent and was concerned that I had not responded back. He was making sure that I knew he was going to be there. I was casual and friendly. I was the perfect combination of witty, interested, and wonderful. It worked! I called to thank my friend. She had helped me work through one of the most important parts of a relationship – the beginning. Once I got through this very cagey part of interpersonal communication and my own debilitating actions, I had set the stage so the relationship could harness its own power.

We had a wonderful date. Deciding to keep it quiet and sweet, we spent time talking and enjoying each other's company. Since the dates were proceeding well, Sam and I felt that we were ready to take this relationship to the next level. This was a big and scary step. However, even with my concerns, the decision proved to be the right one. We connected and enjoyed learning things about each other. It was the beginning of a story that we both hoped to keep writing. I felt an unusual calm and gladness when this man held me in his arms. There was no worry or nerves; it was just right. Our skin and bodies met in all the right places and there was even laughter in the right places as well. It seemed as close to perfect as I could get.

I spent the next day in that haze that I hoped was the start of a happy, new relationship. I was about two feet off the ground in my mind. I smiled in a dazed and rather disarming way. I found myself laughing aloud in the line for coffee. I could even feel the warmth on my neck where he had kissed me. It was all right there in the frontal lobe of my brain and it was intoxicating. I had to call my friends and gush. They were happy for me, and they wanted to live vicariously. Because my friends loved me, they wanted to see me with the right person. They believed that I might have found him but they still reserved the right for an official interview to make a judgment. I went along floating in the dreamy haze of afterglow, when the faucet of reality was turned on me.

I expected some sort of connection. I wanted words of sweetness. What I got was an un-ringing phone that I kept picking up to test to make sure it was working. Minutes clicked by, and I was angry with myself on so many different levels. Why did I get intimate with this man? Everyone knows that it changes everything. Why was Sam not calling to check on me? Why was I expecting him to call? Why did I always lose one sock in the dryer and where does it go?

The vital, strong woman of today was reduced to the shrill, worried woman of, "Why isn't he?" Repeatedly I said, "Why isn't he calling?" The dating game has been stepped up a level; and as a novice, I was out of my league. I called my friend and she told me calmly that this is part of the scheme. Just wait it out and the call I desired would come to fruition. She told me that he would be waiting to call in a couple of days. True to her word, the call came exactly two days later. I was in awe of her foresightedness. I was beginning to believe that she had some sixth or maybe even seventh sense in the understanding of men.

Once Sam finally called, I struggled with many emotions. Part of me wanted to crush him for his unthinking callousness for letting me hang so precipitously for so long. Part of me wanted to scream with delight and tell him, "I like you; I really, really, like you." Part of me wanted to be cool and debonair and amaze him with my wit and intelligence. However, the part that appeared was the one that does not have the fortitude to do any of those things. Instead, the conversation was stilted on my part. Thinking that this man is going to notice the ESP waves that I was sending, I was mildly annoyed when it did not seem to register that I might be a bit miffed. The chasm between the thinking of men and women is so vast. When would I learn that men do not think like women? In fact, the analogy of Mars and Venus is too close, the division between our sexes is more like Venus and Pluto. Shaking my head in irritation, I decided that an enjoyable conversation was much more fun than a one-sided frustration fest, and I allowed the sparkling conversationalist to shine. Sam then made a half-hearted attempt at asking me out. There were no specifics and no organization and I needed both those attributes to be visible. Actually, it was not that obvious whether he had actually asked me out.

I decided that I either needed to lay down the law or decide that I was willing bury my own feelings to keep this man. Surprisingly, I fell into the former category. After understanding that Sam was making all the plans, assumptions, and in essence seemed to have all the control in this blossoming relationship, it was time for my inner woman to make a move. After much hashing over with friends, it was apparent that I was heading right back where I had been for so many years. I was back to what had gotten me married and eventually divorced so many years later. I was becoming the man pleaser. Whatever I thought Sam wanted me to be, I was willing to become. I was thinking of putting my needs secondary to what I thought he wanted or was expecting from me. This was a vital mistake being willing to become the emotional chameleon woman. As this woman, I would be ever ready to change my emotions whenever the man I was interested in changed his. Faster than any reptile on the planet, as this emotional chameleon I could change myself to fit any emotion that Sam may have. I am not sure if changing colors is hard for the chameleons in nature, but for me trying to assimilate to the ever-changing needs of this man or any man had been an exhausting proposition, and I did not want to do it anymore.

I wanted to flex my newly acquired emotional muscles; but my brain went on estrogen autopilot and I began to crumble. What happened to the woman I wanted to be who was strong, vibrant, and would be sure of myself? Where did that ferocious female go who would take what I needed and be sure that it happened on my terms? That woman had conveniently locked herself in the bathroom of my psyche. However, having a good lock pick is beneficial for anyone that has a nervous Nellie in control of her emotional destiny. Once I got the strong woman out of the facilities, it was time to take control of the situation.

I used humor to deflect the truth of my words. After our next date, I told Sam sarcastically that I would expect to hear from him no sooner than two to four days from now given that seemed to be the appropriate period of time for post-coital conversations. He looked at me mystified, and in truth un-knowing, what I was talking about. In stating the obvious, I understood that he really was not sure what to do either. It endeared me to him immediately, but not enough to let him off the hook. I decided that enough was enough, and it was time for the truth. At that juncture, I told Sam that I did not intend to play games, therefore, I had to be honest. I told him that two days of silence was too much time after being intimate with a woman. In fact, probably twelve hours was pushing the limit. I enlightened him that while this may be simply a difference between men and women it was a difference he was going to have to learn to overcome, especially if our pleasant encounters were going to continue. It was obvious that he felt bad. I explained that I was not trying to make him feel bad but only to show him that honesty was a necessity for me. I wondered as I drove away if the death knell had rung for this only-just-begun relationship.

It is always said that when you least expect something, it will happen. I had decided that fate was in control of where this relationship was going. I figured that kismet seemed to have a better handle on where I was to be than I actually did myself. I let go of where, what, and why and decided on just letting it be. I woke up unusually happy and free. I felt that I was actually learning what I needed to be a functional part of the dating society. I enjoyed my day. I enjoyed my life. I enjoyed the being of each moment. In that exact Zen moment, the phone rang and I learned that being myself was the best possible thing I could be.

Sam called me to tell me that this was his post-coital verbal communication with me and that he wanted the bonus points that this action warranted. I laughed and told him that he indeed had scored big with this move. It was at that moment that we both realized that we really liked each other and wanted to know more about who we were. We both had laid ourselves bare in front of the other, not just physically but emotionally, which is a much scarier nudity. By calling, Sam was telling me that he had heard me. He understood what I needed, and he was willing to give it to me. He was showing me in one action that he wanted this to work and see what it was to become. I understood that someone could and would appreciate the what, where, and why that I was. I understood that being myself and trusting the woman that I was becoming was the correct way to be. This man and I were going to be something, for how long was unknown but that was part of the excitement and fear of the situation. That was enough for now. This connection between us was what was going to teach me that anything I believed about myself others would see as well. Perhaps it was impossible to find something that could make me a true believer in myself, but one phone call from the right man at the right time can definitely shine the light on what lay underneath my soul.

CHAPTER TEN

Mediation!

Deciding to move forward with the divorce always seemed to be harder for one person then the other. Taking steps towards a new direction made me happy with the new life that was growing around me. I was ready to further the process on the legal front as well. I did not know if the LCS was ready, but that was not an aspect that I worried about. I saw the man that I had been married to through my clear eyes. The blinders of loving him had come off, and I realized how truly unsuited we were for each other. I did not know if he realized that truth, yet I knew that it was time to take the step that we had been hesitating on. It was time to seek the legal council of "Mr. Who Gets What."

The LCS and I had come to an agreement that we wanted to keep as much of our hard earned cash as possible, so we determined that seeing a mediator would be the right way to go. The concept of mediation is very civilized and a testament to how much divorce occurs today. The mediator was a neutral attorney (I know that seems like an oxymoron, doesn't it?) that would help us divide our assets and items in the fairest possible way. It seemed like a wonderful idea; however, could this feat really take place in a fair and unemotional way?

For our first meeting, the LCS chose the wonderful time of three in the afternoon on a Friday. Anyone who has had to get on a freeway on a Friday afternoon understands the complex problem this created. On Fridays, nothing moves. Helicopters buzz overhead like mosquitoes; cars sit broken down on the side of the road, and people slow down to look at said cars. Road rage is rampant with the culprit's veins popping out of their head. Most motorists tend to glaze over on autopilot, their senses dulled by the fumes coming off the highway.

I allowed myself enough time to reach the office we were meeting at. Even then I was about five minutes late, or so I thought. I called the LCS expecting a lecture on the fine art of time management when he informed me that the appointment was not until a half hour later than I had anticipated. Oh, glee, I was not late. In fact, I was early! It was then that he informed me that he had not even left his office for the appointment. I was in shock. On a good day with absolutely no traffic, it would have taken him about thirty to forty minutes to reach our meeting, but you would need to double that timeframe on a Friday. A smile spread menacingly across my face. I was not going to have to listen to a lecture on time management – I was going to give one. Needless to say, the lecture was not taken with the same open mind that I would have accepted it with.

I used the extra time to fortify myself for the ensuing meeting. I actually had no idea what to expect. That I wanted to move forward legally and start the ball rolling was a given. My mind was a basket of facts and I had not sorted through this basket and separated the whites from the colors. The basket had become rather difficult to lift from the floor as it was heavy with a jumble of fear, anger, and resentments. Sitting in the lobby waiting, I kept thinking that everything could be worked out easily since the LCS and I were being so amenable. I figured that it would be unemotional and dry with facts simply being put to paper. I did not expect any emotions. So imagine my surprise when I realized that emotion was sitting in the chair next to mine.

Once the LCS arrived and we started the meeting, facts were bandied around freely. Of course, the LCS was overly prepared with budget sheets, research papers, and receipts from ten years ago. I, on the other hand, was woefully unprepared on all fronts. I had the few bills I had paid in the last few months. I had my very small pay stubs from my very small job. I had a soda. That was the arsenal that I had armed myself with for this meeting. I was wearing no armor. I did not have chain mail. I was an open target for reality.

As the mediator started talking and the facts hovered over the monetary issue, I started thinking wild thoughts. My first thought was that if the LCS had realized how much this was going to cost, he would have never left me. Money, of course, was his first love. The other thoughts were angry thoughts. How dare the LCS cause this complete upheaval of my life at the time where I was supposed to be enjoying what we had put together over the years? I felt anger rising up into my chest. I was becoming more irate the more the money issues were discussed. I never really had cared about the money because the money had always been there. When I began to understand that my woeful salary at my new job was not going to even keep me in toilet tissue, I started to get mad. Damn him! The LCS had started all this. If his stupid mid-life crisis had not occurred, I would be living unhappily in wedded semi-bliss. I would be like most other married couples; sometimes loving their husbands and sometimes wanting to run over them with a car.

It was his fault. I blamed him. I was feeling all the classic woman-being-divorced emotions. I felt that because he had instigated the whole situation, he should be left with nothing but a pot to piss in. He was the reason that at thirty-eight years old I was going to have to face what I had always hoped to avoid. I was going to have to fend for my children and myself. No one was going to be there to bail me out. My mom and dad were not going to take care of me. My husband was not going to take care of me. I was not going to win the lottery. I was going to have to do it all by myself.

What did that mean to me? That meant that my lifestyle of shopping and enjoying the comforts of being upper-middle class were going to be gone. Gone would be the monthly facials. I would not be getting my nails done whenever I wanted. I could not go away on spa weekends with the girls. I was going to have to pinch a lot of pennies. While I knew that I could do this and still have a nice life, I was still angry. I was sounding petty but I did not grasp that my life had become just that, petty.

It was a big moment when I comprehended why I had been stomping around grumbling into my designer lipstick. I was scared. I had been the pampered only child, went straight into a marriage with an established man, and now I was a divorced woman who would be trying to make ends meet. One night while walking around my neighborhood, I watched all the families bar-b-queuing or playing at the park and my anger level elevated. Although I knew I was happier without the LCS, I was now an outcast. I was not asked to parties that were stocked with married couples. I felt like the Jezebel woman. The problem was that I was not the person that had created this new existence. The blame lay elsewhere as far as I was concerned, but did it? I was not sure anymore who was truly at fault for the dissolving of our marriage. I watched television shows where young newlyweds gushed love and fidelity for one another and I heard the cynic in me say, just wait for another eleven years. You will be singing a different tune, or would they? Would they be able to keep the spark and love alive in their marriage or would their marriage go the way of the fifty percent that ended in divorce?

I knew I was to blame for the failure of my marriage just as much as the LCS was. I had walked away years ago from the work it would have taken to create a strong and loving marriage. It all had gotten too hard. So instead of putting the hours in years ago, I left the remodeling for later. I figured that I could always find a good contractor to help us shore up the foundation of our marriage. The tools would be ready whenever they were needed. The problem was that by the time I understood that renovation was imperative, the LCS was already looking at a new address.

Facing certain behaviors in myself was not much fun. I could go through my life knowing things about myself and being able to cover up the not so desirable qualities with excuses or blame. Yet when I had no one else to blame, I had to start examining myself in the mirror.

At breakfast with a friend of mine, I was whining about my not being able to get facials and pedicures as much as I liked. She stated that she never had gotten those things; and not because she did not want them, but because she knew they were not important. I, on the other hand, had expected them. Being taken care of for most of my life had made me a pampered and spoilt woman with more than enough intelligence but not enough drive. I had been sitting on my tasseled pillow too long. My job as a mother was challenging, but I had gotten good at it so the challenge was minimal. I had not yet reached the point where I was ready to dive back into the fray. I wanted to at some point but I planned to slip slowly off my pillow and not have it yanked out from underneath me. I realized that I probably would not receive much sympathy from those who had never sat on the puffy pillow; but no matter where you rest your bum, the loss of a marriage and its life was going to be felt. In facing the new existence that was being thrust upon me, I realized that I had some hard lessons to learn.

I already knew that patience was high up on my lesson plan. What amazed me was how many other attributes I needed to work on. Now was the time to learn how to restrain myself. Over the years, I had used shopping as a placebo for whenever I was sad, depressed, or upset. When I felt bad, I would go out and shop and get that high that comes from spending money. Yet I now appreciated that those highs did not last. What happened was that I had lots of stuff and nothing in the bank. This could not continue, because now I needed that money in the bank to buy serious items like breakfast, lunch, and dinner. It was time to grow up.

I had always left the money handling to the LCS. I paid the bills every week but only because I was tired of being berated for my overspending. By paying the bills myself, I did not have to hear all the cussing and swearing at my purchasing habits. All the management of our future money was in the hands of my very conservative mate. He did right by us in that avenue. He was safe and was always looking to the end. That was just another glaring example of how very different we were.

Now I was in charge of my future and the future of my children. I was woefully unprepared for this. I had no idea how to watch the markets; and in all honesty, I had no interest (pardon my pun) in doing so. I felt frozen because there was so much to learn, know, and be responsible for that I did not know where to start. I have to say that there was one moment when I thought that a loveless marriage might not be a bad idea if I just did not have to go out and learn all the things that I did not want to learn. However, that did not sit right with the strong woman that lurked behind the insecure child that was my psyche. The strong woman was trying to take over the child and was succeeding on many levels. Yet that child could at times have temper tantrums and grab the credit card causing all sort of havoc in the new chapter of my life. It was my job to take control of this child and put her in a time out.

I did not need any more hair, make-up, or body products. That was apparent by my friend's comment that I had sort of a hairspray bar on my vanity. I did not need any more clothes since I was happily filling up both sides of the walk-in closet. I did not need any more food. I had a house filled with toys, furniture, necessary and unnecessary items. I was well off and in no dire need. I was lucky. I decided that to stay in my house and keep my kids stable was going to take vast changes on their mother's way of living. I was resolved to make those changes. I would become the type of person who understood that going without can be great and character building. I was going to be able to show my children that things worth doing often times take sacrifice. It was important to learn that going without or learning to know what was important was a quality that would be one of the best lessons they would ever learn.

Chapter Eleven

When do we get to Heaven?

As a newly divorced woman, I needed to create some alliances. I needed support. I found this support with women in my same situation. There is a kindred spirit in the woman divorced. Every woman that has been through a divorce identifies with the emotions I was experiencing. They had been where I was. It became evident that there were different tiers to the divorced woman's life. There were newbies, of which I was one. I was just entering my separation and beginning my divorce proceedings. There were the mid-level "functioning and beginning to enjoy life again" divorcees. These women had been through the worst and were starting to believe that their life would be better. The time line seemed to be about year for this stage. Lastly, there were the divorcees who had made it past the two-year mark and were moving on successfully with their lives. Being new to this whole game, I looked at the two-year mark as the gateway to heaven. For some reason the mark of 730 days was where I would seemingly be able to put everything I had learned together and start building myself up again. Two friends that had hit this mark were inspirational in the fury of their new lives.

As a newbie, I started simple. I had just lost my husband, and my relationship with Sam had ended. I knew that the bar scene seemed to be not getting me too far on the road to dating. I followed the advice of my friends higher on the divorce tier. They recommended on-line dating; and while the concept of on-line dating seems in theory fantastic, it did seem to defy rational thought. My first impression was that it was like a supermarket for men. I could select all the attributes that I wanted from a vast array of acceptable and willing men. While this might seem heavenly, being able to see a laundry list of the available men was not the nirvana I had anticipated. To begin dating on-line I must have an incredible photo. First lesson, not one man that was walking on this earth that I would truly want to meet would meet me for coffee if he did not see what I looked like. In all fairness, I would not do it either. Have I established that what I looked like was important? Duh!

However, when I surveyed the competition on-line before I submitted my profile, I was dumbfounded. It looked like the who's who of a glamour magazine shot. There were women there so beautiful that I looked at them and questioned, "She can't get a date?" I wanted to cry in my bed for about three days. People spent large quantities of hard-earned cash on these photos. It appeared that if I did not have backlighting and a professional makeup job, then I had better find some good books to read.

Balking at all obvious needs for high quality photo equipment, I decided after a few too many lemon drops one night, that my digital camera on my phone would take a completely adequate and enticing photo. I would be taking said photo myself. You can only imagine the results. However, I wanted to be dating soon, since I felt a need to fill the job of man in my life quickly before I could notice that the position had been vacated. I posted my crooked and unsmiling photo and waited, and waited, and waited, and waited. Finally, I received a response. Not exactly what I was looking for though. It was an over seventy-five year-old wearing a cowboy hat and suspenders. "Did it hurt falling from heaven?" he asked. Hmm, maybe I did need a new picture. I changed the picture. The hits on my site went up, but that was about all. What was I doing wrong?

The answer was easy; I was one in a bazillion women out there trying to grab a man's gnat-like attention. I had one second to snare him from the bombshell three pictures down from mine. The main problem in my opinion was that the on-line sites were specifically visual. Men were looking at the pictures while only sometimes taking the time to read the profiles. How could I compete with so many women with all the same agenda? There was no eye contact. There was no witty and sparkling conversation. There was no chance for my personality to attract someone. There was not a chance for the man to like the way I smiled. Flirting with the chosen men and being able to intrigue them with only email banter seemed futile. Romance was not part of this equation. This was dating at its down and dirtiest.

Even if I actually connected with someone and decided to take it to the next level, one of two things happened. We would chat on email and then one day I would never hear from them again; or I would meet them and find that everything they advertised on the site was exactly what they were not. That became the longest cup of coffee ever consumed.

Romance, love, and intimacy were not for the internet. I have heard stories of people meeting, falling in love, and getting married after meeting on the internet. However, these people may be urban legends since I have never met one of these blissfully happy couples. I would like to see some statistics on success in the dating world via the internet. My fear of meeting people on the internet stemmed from the idea that anyone can portray themselves any way they want and how would I really know them?

I started thinking, what had I really known of my spouse before we married. We dated for a bit, moved in together, and then we were engaged. I thought I knew him. I went through his underwear drawer and found his stashed soft porn, so it must be all he was hiding. Based on this marginal detective work, I decided to walk into a marriage with a complete stranger and hope that I had made a good choice. I guess I had been lucky because for many years our marriage seemed to go okay and I thought we were happy. Then slowly, day by day, the marriage shifted. He became his job and I became the home and all of its contents. The excitement I used to feel when he walked in the door changed after we had children. Instead of anticipating seeing my spouse, I was just happy to have another adult to talk to. I bombarded my spouse with news about my stressful day with the children before he had a chance to get his other foot in the door. It sent a message to him that I was not able to cope with the job I had taken on. I had forgotten about the bonding time that was needed between us to keep our communication alive. When my spouse got home, he wanted to have a chance to sit down and detach from his world outside. Instead, his other role of father and armchair psychologist to my challenges as a mother was thrust upon him. Slowly he started to resent me. We seemed to be in different places heading different directions. This disconnect happened so subtly that by the time I understood there was a problem, it seemed to be too late.

Growth takes place in every individual. Maturation can cause a deterioration of the marriage. I grew up as I aged. I was taking care of the kids, the home, while meeting the needs of my spouse, and that was immense responsibility. My husband had his own weights of responsibility that he carried. Yet we never discussed how these issues were causing a rift in us. My kids started to grow up and I felt that it allowed me to grow too. Once they started school, I felt my spouse starting to look at me like, "Ready to start earning some cash now?" For some reason he felt that even though I stayed home and watched the kids, I was not really working. In his opinion since I did not have a pay stub attached to my role, I had been lounging around eating candy while watching daytime television instead of raising our children through their formative years. Something he did not conceive of was that I was ready to start again too. I wanted to feed my mind. I wanted to take classes and pursue my interests. I began to wonder what career I could have that would allow time for laundry and dishes that needed to be washed. While my job as a mother was becoming easier, the task of deciding what I wanted to be when I grew up was far more daunting.

Men seem to go in the opposite direction of maturity as they get older. They seem to start worrying about their bald spots and paunches. They go to the gym more and buy cool cars. They ogle younger woman and wonder if their wives would be willing to get boob jobs. All they seem to think about is how they are stuck, trapped, and chained to this older and becoming-wiser woman. They revert to high school where all that mattered was having a cool car and a hot chick.

Once again, my spouse and I seemed to be at opposite ends of our growth spectrum, and not able to see eye to eye. Many couples can weather this very tough spot of marriage.

Many others cannot. Being one of the latter, I decided that this whole process had happened for a reason. Being left was part of my life lessons. That lesson was not so that I could find a new guy to become the prince that I obviously had not picked correctly the first time around. The reason for this incredible upheaval of my life, was for me to learn about me. I was the reason that this happened. The cosmos and the powers that be decided that it was my time to be free. It didn't make sense, but in all honesty, when faced with life's biggest lessons, do they ever really make sense? This change in my life had happened so I could find not a new man, but so I could find a new woman - me.

It is an interesting concept that I had to be weak before I could be strong. I have heard it said that you must experience one extreme of an emotion before you can truly understand the other extreme. I believe that this statement was blaringly true in my life's example.

The saddest day in my life was when my mother died. Losing the one person that had carried, borne, and loved me unconditionally, was the most devastating event of my life. It broke my heart. I never physically understood this statement, until I sat at my mother's memorial service and listened to my six-year-old daughter talk about how much she was going to miss her grandma. My heart muscle felt torn in two that day.

I have watched people in agony physically, mentally, and spiritually and like them have asked the question, "Why?" When that question is not answered, I find it incredible that our human spirit is strong enough to pick itself up and con-tinue to feel again. I knew it may take time, tears, and days spent in bed eating ice cream, but I would get up one day and feel the sun on my face. That is the testament to what being human is all about.

After a summarily bad day, capped off with no emails or icebreakers from my on-line dating, I recognized that I was putting the stress on the wrong aspect in my life. I was missing the message. I needed to be looking at me. I needed to build myself up and start growing again. I gave advice to a friend, telling her that if she did not love herself she was never going to be able to be out in the world, let alone find someone who would love her. I absolutely needed to take my own advice on this point. I needed to love myself. I did not need to have a man to love me to make me worth something. I did not need someone's approval as to what I was doing in my life. I did not need to be taken care of. I could do all these things myself.

I decided that when I had found myself and my place, then the man I was waiting for could come to me. I needed to create the glow of happiness, stillness, and pride that would be a homing beacon for the man that was my prince. With that in mind, I began each day letting go and telling the powers that be to take me where I was supposed to be that day.

Is anyone getting nauseous yet? I know it all seems very smelly incense and lighted candles, but it was true and right. That does not mean that I did not feel sometimes that I was the greatest hag in the valley when not one response to my emails was returned. I am human. Yet by knowing that I was going to get through all of this and be stronger for it, I was able to handle that rejection a bit better and a little sooner than before.

My friends and family were the cornerstone to making it through this time. They were there to hold me up and love me. They told me I was terrific and inspirational. They had me to dinner and went with me to movies. They supported me and made me feel that I was never alone, even when I was standing in my kitchen by myself eating peanut butter out of the jar. Knowing that I could make a phone call and have someone to talk, cry, or laugh with me, was the best life preserver that I could have had.

Heaven appears to be at the top of a great staircase. I was on the bottom of the stairs. Each day I was a step closer. Sometimes I slipped on a step and hurt the ball of my foot. On some days, I could almost hear those pearly gates squeaking. On other days, it seemed like the staircase would never end. Heaven was there everyday. It was in the kiss of my children when they went to bed. It was in the orange of a beautiful night sky. It was in the feeling when I met someone and the butterflies started to flutter. It was in the feeling that I was a wonderful, strong, and capable person that had created an existence all my own. Heaven was where I was every minute, I just needed to have a look around.

The sliding scale of Hell

As you learn to maneuver through each day, many bumps and turns come up. There were untold emotions that bounced me up and down at any given moment. Through each day, a low hum of anger seemed to be just below the boiling point. This anger was usually directed at the LCS. The anger came from many different faucets. When each faucet was only turned on a trickle, I was able to keep the sink of emotion from overflowing. Yet life was not always kind to me as I was trying to keep the stopper in my emotional sink. There was always some sort of event that came up: birthday parties for the kids, holidays, or a chance meeting with the LCS. Let's take a moment to dissect these events for further growth potential.

Birthday parties for my children should have been uproarious and wonderful occasions that made me smile and laugh. Yet when I had to face that event with the LCS in attendance, it put a completely different spin on the frivolity. I started out smiling while being the gracious and wonderful hostess. I felt I could handle this situation. I was the bigger and more mature person. I glided through the party with the grace of a swan. I poured drinks, mostly for me, and made sure that all my guests were enjoying themselves. I took special care with the LCS. I wanted to show him and myself, that I could handle this extremely uncomfortable situation. I was sure that everyone would marvel at the fantastic job that I was doing keeping the atmosphere light and jovial; but just like the clown's red nose at the party, the strain of the relationship was blaringly fake. Halfway through the party the LCS started acting like himself. The irritations became like sandpaper in my ears. I was finding it hard not to stab him with the cake cutter. By the time the clean up occurred, I wanted to kick him in his inconsiderate hindquarters. Why was he here? Why did I have to keep seeing him, over and over again? Why didn't he just move to China and make my life easier? I held it together until the guests had left and the children were abed; then I let him have it. I did not come right out and say, "I am still so hurt and angry at you for effectively destroying my life that I can barely stay in the same room with you." I picked at something stupid and trivial. I commented on his clothing. I bashed his speech pattern. I found any way to pay back the hurt and pain that his behavior had created in my life.

What was the pain and suffering? It was being single at this age and having to go and start all over again. Even if I was happier without him, I still wanted him to suffer for what he had put me through. Tit for tat was alive and well in this arena. Inevitably, I acted ridiculous and childish, but it felt good for the moment. Reverting to our old married form, I sent several arrows his way. He countered with his own arrows. He left in a huff, and I huffed around the house finishing the clean up. Immaturity and emotionalism had taken the upper hand once again. Did I feel better? No, I felt worse because I had just let the faucet overflow, and the gunk in the disposal had spilled over into my new life. I too easily fell back into the couple mentality for the moment. Then after I took the time to calm down and clean up the party paraphernalia and my emotions, I recognized that it was all for nothing. I was happier without the LCS. I was living a life that I needed. So what caused me to become so out of control, when I was forced to deal with him?

"Forced to deal with him" was the phrase that created the anger. When I *had* to do anything, it made it hard to swallow. If someone made me eat ten pounds of chocolate, I would be irritated. So having to spend time with someone who had told me that I was not worth spending time with when we were married, caused in me a bit of rankling. What did I do? My kids were not going to stop having birthdays so that I would not have to see the LCS. I had to find a common ground. Where was that ground? Panama?

I found that the emotional faucets started flowing every time I was obligated to spend time with the LCS. With the holidays approaching, I found other emotions being stirred up as well. The first Easter after the break-up, I felt particularly angry. Not only did I have to do all preparations (that was nothing new), but also I had to spend the whole day with the LCS pretending that I wanted him to be there. I did not want to. I gave invitations because I was trying to be kind. I wanted to create a festive atmosphere for the children, but I grasped that I had not been motivated to decorate the house. I was not creating that happy-go-lucky feeling that usually accompanied these events. The atmosphere was forced, and I felt more alone having to be with someone that had hurt me. I focused on the kids and they enjoyed themselves, but I felt that in some way I was fostering false hopes for them. When the LCS and I were together, I could see how the kids watched our every move as if to see if we were getting back together. As we settled into the rest of the afternoon after the requisite Easter brunch, I could not stop the sad feeling taking hold of my heart. I felt like an orphan. I felt abandoned and alone. I felt in a limbo state. I knew then that I had to make some decisions, and events had to change.

I needed to start anew making my own celebrations. I needed to separate myself from what we used to do as a family. This was a new era in my life. I was in charge, and that feeling of not having to ask permission of anyone was a new feeling that I did not know what to do with. It was time to set expectations of the holidays and create boundaries that would not sabotage my new life. I needed to tell the LCS that he could take the kids for part of the day, and I would take them for the other part. Our celebrations would have to be separate. It was not up to me to create the fun for him. I was not responsible for how he handled his life. I was only responsible for my children and myself. I had made his life comfortable for so long, that I did not know how to stop doing it. Friends told me that I was being too nice and that he needed to lie in the bed he had made; but taking care of the LCS and my family was all that I knew how to do. It was not my place anymore to be responsible for his happiness, but I did not know how to end the behaviors.

I had to think in the manner of one that was free. It was a difficult concept since I had never truly been free in my entire life. I became conscious of the fact that going from my parents into the safety of an established man, I had never challenged myself. I had allowed the safety of money and comfort to soften my drive and ambition. The drive and ambition was beginning to awaken in me, and I wanted to follow through with where it would lead me. All this was new to someone who had coasted through their life, letting others make most of the decisions for them. I had to trust myself. I needed to learn to trust my instincts and know that whatever outlines I would make would be the right plan of attack. It meant that sometimes I might make mistakes. It meant that I was going to stumble and have to get up and brush myself off with more knowledge acquired. I felt that I was going to be all right. I would make it even if a tough road lay ahead. As I grew stronger in this blossoming power, the LCS became more and more threatened. The fighting began again in earnest, as he started to realize that what had held me to him before was dissipating, and he was no longer going to control me.

Many seeds germinated in my head during this holiday season. I started to think more about what I was going to do with my future. I started to see more and more coincidences occurring, at least they seemed like coincidences. For example, I decided to plan my first vacation alone with the children. I could not decide on anything. I looked at Canada. I thought about England. I browsed through the cruise schedules. The cruises were what I was looking for. The kids loved going on the Alaska cruise the year before. This vacation would afford time with the kids having fun in the sun, and some alone time for myself. It would be a perfect mix and balance. Yet, when I looked at the prices, I felt that I had to run for the phone to get an okay from the LCS. At that very moment, the call came from the cruise line. They had the cruise I wanted, on the days I wanted to travel, and the piece de resistance was that they had one cabin left. I gave my credit card information and booked it. It felt liberating.

The process was continuing. I was traveling further down that road. I was becoming the woman, mother, and person that I wanted to be. I was expanding my spirit and creating a new and improved version of myself. I was working through my self-esteem issues, and I was beginning to see that I was a terrific woman. I began to see myself through others' eyes. It was rather enlightening. I was moving out from the hell of not knowing to the place of understanding. I was not going to be in this holding pattern forever. I would come up and out of what was the rubble of my marriage; and when I emerged, I would be a solid countenance of womanhood. One thing I understood was I was not alone. There were so many women going through this same process. It was with that realization that a completely new world opened up for me.

Learning what to be!

fter going through the emotional rollercoaster of the first few months of being left, I decided that living in an alcoholic haze was not a long-term way of life. I changed my outlook and was becoming infinitely stronger. I appreciated that I could be alone on a weeknight and be okay with that. I tested my newfound strength by consciously staying home on a Saturday night and did not become a pile of goo. In fact, I actually enjoyed the freedom and empowerment of being alone with my choice of movie and a bowl of popcorn. I had crossed the finish line of individuality. I had a single life filled with fun and frivolity. However, most of my friends were married people with no attractive and eligible bachelor friends seeking dates, so it fell to my divorcee friends to help develop my social calendar.

My friend, who was part of the same singles organization that I was a member of called and asked if I would go to an event with her just to see if the program had improved in the least since our last foray. Even though I had not been impressed with their dating pool, she convinced me to sign up for a crab feed on a boat. The idea seemed a bit cruel since we would be throwing our shells over the side of the boat. I could not help thinking about the crabs just sitting around doing their crab things at the bottom of the bay and having their friends' various shell parts falling on top of them. Having no expectations, because by now I knew better, we entered the boat. It was apparent from the very first second that things in this organization had not improved. My friend told me that I was now her date for the afternoon. We picked, poked, sawed, clawed, and sucked the crab out of its shell. I was working diligently on my crab and trying not to make eye contact with the guy in front of me, when the meat I was trying to extricate from the shell flipped off my fork and into the his wine glass. I was mortified. Apologies gushed from my mouth. He did not seem extremely phased by the entire event. He picked up his wine glass, took a sip, and pronounced that the "crabernet sauvignon" was delicious. I looked at my friend and said, "When this boat stops, we are out of here." After sitting quietly through the meal while the "crabernet sauvignon" guy sent crab everywhere with half of his meal ending up in his hair, the boat mercifully landed. My friend and I said our goodbyes and raced off the ship. Once hitting dry land, we looked at each other and said, "Thank God for you!"

This was the truth. Thank God for my compadres in pain. We were all suffering together; and instead of crying, we were laughing. That was a wonderful and telling event. I was laughing more and crying less. All these women were helping me to get through each day and ascertain that being alone was better than being with the "crabernet sauvignon" guy or the LCS. I had more fun with these women than I did with most of the men I had dated so far. It was time to get them all together and create a force, an army of strength and humor.

I decided that I would start a support group for all the women I had met that were living through their own private metamorphosis. There were women of all stages in the process of divorce, and each of them had something important to share. What if we all got together to form a group that could help each other out when were sad, lonely, hurt, crushed, jubilant, or all of the above? Why not bring all these women together that I had met and see what brewed? It could not hurt to share each other's pain. It would be like an AA meeting for the divorced, left, or separated.

Women that have gone or were going through a divorce are a breed all their own. The divorced woman does not really have a place in the society fiber. This is amazing given that there are so many of us. However, I felt that I did not really belong anywhere. My spouse was no longer there and my family unit was blown sky high. As a divorcee I did not feel great being in the married world of school drop-offs, dinner parties, holiday celebrations and just about anywhere that I used to hang around. It was a strange feeling of belonging, yet not belonging.

I tried to explain this to one of my married friends. She felt sad that this was how I felt. Even though my married friends were enjoying my newfound freedom and living a bit vicariously through my exploits, they still were glad that they had their husband's cold feet on them in the middle of the night. Part of me wished that I had icy toes or even sharp toenails cutting up my legs every night. I missed that companionship that had been there for so long and was supposed to be there until death do we part. I did not miss the anger, resentment, or general bad mood that accompanied the steely-knifed toes. Because this absence of malice far out shadowed the need for frozen toes on my legs, I was able to make it through the next day, week, month, or even year. Yet it was a tricky place to be and really only one other type of person truly understands where I was and what I was feeling, another divorcee.

There are support groups for every ailment, condition, and problem that you could ever encounter yet not one for the divorced women. We women were supposed to be like the children of the fifties, seen and not heard. Yet every woman I had met had plenty to say and no one to say it to.

I was not creating a group that was going to sit around and bash men. Well honestly, there might be a little bashing going on. This group was going to be about building stronger women. We would create new friendships and find people to connect with that would understand our specific pain and be there to help us get through it. This group would provide someone to eat chocolate with on the nights we did not have the kids and were feeling lonely. Someone to go and sing karaoke with that would not laugh if you sang off-key. We would have support for those holidays when we felt abandoned and alone. This group would fill a need that was not being met in our lives.

I rounded up my friends, they rounded up their friends, and by the time it was done, we had twelve women interested in being part of the group. I started writing down monikers to use as our name. Women No Longer Angry – WNLA. Yuck! Women Are Laughing – WAL. I don't think so. Women in Transition – yes! WIN! That was it!

I put it to a vote of the new attendees and they were completely enthusiastic. Perhaps the special lemonade concoction I had created helped aid their decision making. This was not your kid's juice box, I will tell you. There was vodka involved, of course.

The name was chosen. We were women in transition. My, that was true. More than just divorced women were interested in this group. Our attendance was widespread. There were single women who had never been married. A woman who had been married and her spouse had died. There were women from all stages of the divorced process. There were women who were still married but questioning who and what they were. It was empowering and wonderful to see this group forming into action. The women were intelligent with different insights into how they perceived this world and how it related to them. We all had something to learn from one another and it only took one evening to find that out. I went to work. I developed a second meeting and a third; and before I knew it, we were a full-fledged support group with monthly activities. It was going to be fantastic to watch these women grow and help one another.

I truly believe that there is a very important reason why so many divorces are occurring now. With the wealth available to many women, we set ourselves up for this potential loss of self. We start to become mommies, carpoolers, cooks – of the short order variety, house cleaners, laundry wenches, worker bees, and lastly, wives. No one can do all that every day and keep that smile on their face without either alcohol or a wide variety of pills.

Women today are supposed to be it all. We must have the cleanest house, the best dressed kids, and we should be thin and beautiful. We must have a wonderful marriage, our dog should be adequately walked, and our children should be excelling at school. We should never tire. We should be able to talk about politics at the drop of a hat. And we should satisfy every sexual whim of our husband. All this is on a very low intake level of sleep, affection, caressing, communication, or pats on the back.

What happens to the person that we used to be? What happens to the person we want to be? Nothing happens.

We stay stuck in this place and feel that we should be happy with what we have because it certainly could be worse. While women know and understand that, we still cannot help but resent the fact that the individual that we were, was now lost under piles and piles of laundry.

I had a friend so overwhelmed by this issue, she did not feel like she was going to be able to hold it together much longer. She went to see a doctor whom she had never met, who said, "Where did that girl go that used to be you?" She told me it was as if someone had thrown cold water on her. That one sentence gave absolute and perfect clarity to what she was feeling. Where *was* that girl? What happened to the dreams and the desires that she once had? Why did many women today give up their power to placate and please everyone else?

I told my friend that I believed that everyone has lessons to learn in this lifetime. How we learn them is partially up to us and partially up to the powers that surround us. She looked at me as if I was going to bring out my crystal ball and conjure up some deceased relatives. I told her that we all have angels that follow us around and help us with decisions. If we listen to those angels then our lessons are easier and make more sense. If we do not listen and continue to try to control every outcome of our lives, we will constantly be let down and end up facing a wall of disappointment that cannot be scaled.

I do not believe in coincidences. I had been reading an author that stated that coincidences do not exist. Everything that happened to me happened for a reason. Everything, down to what traffic light I made, and if I dropped my keys, put me in a place I was supposed to be. Many aspects of what had happened to me seemed like coincidences; for example, finding the cell phone bill of the LCS. How my trip to Italy fell into place. How meeting Nicco had been many small steps up a ladder to deciding that my marriage was over. Being introduced to new friends that were entering new phases in their lives too. None of this was by chance. Meeting all these women and helping them get stronger was making my self stronger too. The same aspects were happening in their lives. It just took a different light shining on them to make them appear. We all took turns using the light to help each other discover the woman underneath.

At this point that I started to decipher why I did not seem to be meeting many men. It was not that I had some very bad body odor. It was not that I was in the running for the carnival sideshow. It was because I had something to do. I was supposed to create this group; and by doing that, create this person that gave more than she took. I was supposed to bring these women together to empower womanhood. I read a book about an ancient culture that would have women getting ready to start their cycle go into a tent and spend three weeks there with other women. The elder women shared the secrets of how important being a woman was to their way of life. They learned that women needed to rally together in a supportive and nurturing way. So many times these days, communication between women is superficial and a lot of backbiting occurs. We women need to become conscious that every woman needs every other woman. A bond can form that creates an invincible strength for womankind.

That was my job now. I would follow this path until the journey was played out. It appeared that nothing romantically was going to happen. It was not my time or place to be involved. I knew in my heart that a special person was waiting in the wings. That was what made it so hard, knowing that they were close but not reachable, at least not right now. I let the idea of a relationship simmer and I worked on getting our group together.

It was great to see the excitement and enthusiasm that the women showed. The membership grew. Women who were married and dealing with husbands out of work wanted to come. Women who where just not sure of their place and purpose in their world wanted to be there. Everyone was welcome. Everyone checked her judgments and beliefs at the door. We wanted to form a unit. A unit that would be a base for all of us to step over the fence to see what was coming in our lives.

We were all working to make ourselves better. We asked the tough questions like, where are we supposed to be going and how do we get there? Everyone had different destinations but we all wanted to be on the same flight, especially if the beverage cart was coming down our aisle. It was fun to laugh and joke about where our lives were going and where we had come from. There were enough stories to pack the longest book. The wonderful part of getting together to discuss the stories was the fact that the anger and sadness started to dissipate and the humor and understanding came to the front. When others are supportive, it makes even the deepest and saddest issue bearable.

During this time bits and pieces of hope kept showering down on me. A friend was sitting in an airport before her flight. She was discussing a problem her sister was having. The sister's mother-in-law kept saying that her sister's body weight did not match her height. My friend's sister was lamenting that her mother-in-law was in fact saying she was fat. As they discussed the issue at hand, they gathered their belongings and headed to the gate. Waiting to give their boarding passes, the attractive man that had been sitting across from them ran up and gave my friend a bag. In the bag was a magazine, a box of chocolates, and a postcard that stated she was exactly the right weight for her height and his phone number. After talking and setting up a date, they fell in love; and five weeks after they met the attractive man asked my friend's parents for her hand in marriage.

Another friend of mine went on a business trip. She got on the rental car bus and sat down. She felt a jolt of electricity shoot through her when she looked into the beautiful eyes of the man sitting next to her. They chatted the whole way to the rental car hub. There he gave her his card under the guise that she should call about some pertinent information he had. She took the card and climbed into her car. She knew that she had just met the man of her dreams and was now driving away from him. She called her girlfriend and said, "What do I do?" After a week, she finally emailed him. Being that he was a pilot, he was flying into her area the next weekend. They spent that weekend talking and getting to know each other. I am now helping her plan her wedding!

Armed with this hope and the true romantic soul that I have, I forged on in the day-to-day world and the dating world. Let down often in both places, I still managed to get up every day and learn. I managed to finish the items on my "to do" list. I managed to help others. I managed to help myself at times too. I kept growing and growing, all the time continuing to find myself.

CHAPTER FOURTEEN

This is me... can I help you?

I had a job. It was nice to work and use the mental capacity on the other side of my brain that had been lying dormant for a while. I enjoyed dressing up a bit and getting ready in the morning. I made myself lunch along side my children's lunch. I was feeling competent and grown-up. I got the kids to school, the dog to the dog play place, a cappuccino to go, and myself to work all by nine o'clock. It was sometimes a challenge. Some days it was a breeze.

When I got to work, I left the Mom-hat in the car. I was the professional ready to attack the corporate world. I was ready to take the sales galaxy by storm and become the Tony Robbins of meeting planning. It was invigorating and exciting. I came in fired up and was happy by the end of the day that I did not end up fired. I made it through one week. Then I passed one month. It was incredible. I was working and loving it.

I was managing the house, homework, feeding the kids, and miraculously I was not failing. So the house wasn't a picture of organization. Okay, there were some dishes left in the sink in the morning. I was still able to keep it a relatively attractive home. It created a strong sense that I was going to be able to succeed as this divorced woman of thirty-eight. I was empowered. I understood some of the needs that I had been missing during my marriage. By going to work, I received a tangible item at the end of a workweek – a paycheck. I knew I was doing my job because someone was paying me. When I stayed home, I never got a paycheck. No one came and gave me a progress report. There was no probation period. I never was sure that I was doing a good job. My kids were alive, that was a good sign. No one had gotten food poisoning from my cooking. That was a plus. However, other than a good Mother's Day present, I did not get many pats on the back.

I have heard from working women that it is easier to go to work than to stay home with the kids. I grasped why they were right. At work, I could go to the bathroom by myself without someone knocking on the door incessantly. My boss was not going to shove papers under the door to have me look at them while I was peeing. She was not going to stand outside the door and knock to ask how long I was going to be. I could go in the bathroom and put on lipstick. I could wash my hands extra long and contemplate the one stall factor in women's public bathrooms, because no one was going to come and get me. It was a small and perfect moment.

Working also allowed me to be with other people, and in my case, a friend that I had not seen for a while. It was great to work and share a laugh or two with her. It was the best of both worlds. I had a lunch hour, which was a wonderful concept for a stay-at-home mom, because I actually sat and ate a lunch that was mine. I was not eating the leftover crusts off stale sandwiches. I was not finishing the last bit of mushy banana that was left on the plate. I could have a salad that was crunchy, satisfying, and healthy. While eating this delectable lunch I could either read a book if I happened to be eating by myself (which also was a blissful concept) or I could chat my way through an hour with a colleague. It was great to be able to connect to that part of the person that I used to be.

Work was one of the aspects that became foremost to creating the new me. It helped with the ability to believe that my life was going on and I was in complete control. As I rounded a year, I was at the height of my optimism. I was busy. I had friends. I was going places and doing new things. I was a blur of activity. When I got home from work, dinner out, or after running the kids to their many activities, I was too tired to really look at myself and see what I did not want to see.

Inevitably, the day came when I had to look at the woman in the mirror. My children went with the LCS to visit their grandparents over a vacation. At first, I was thrilled with the idea of five whole days to do whatever I wanted. I did not have to work. I did not need to cook dinner or help anyone with his or her homework. I was going to be carefree and hopefully involved with a bit of romance to boot. I had been talking to a man for a while, so I played the disastrous expectation game. I put it in my head that I would be able to spend a weekend getting to know this newest love to enter my life.

As the weekend dawned, everything turned topsy-turvy. The new love did not materialize. My friends all had found either their loves or roads out from the loneliness. I found myself completely alone. This time there were no beautiful museums or international cuties to ogle. There was just my house, my dog, and me. I had convinced myself that I had everything under control. I was amazed how fast I could go from the strong person that I thought I was to a puddle of ooze and tears. I tried to find things to do. I planted plants. I went to the movies. I worked out. I walked the dog. Yet no matter what I did, I still had to catch the glimpse of myself in the mirror. There was no one else there, just me.

On this particular weekend, the friends that would have rallied around me to help ease me out of this rather large pot of self-pity were off with their own blossoming romances. Every time I turned on the television, there was a new love story. Finally, I was unable to keep the stiff upper chin any longer. There was no reason to keep up appearances as the only company I had was the dog. I let it go. I cried and cried and cried. Then after blowing my nose, I cried again. I yelled and screamed. I cursed and pleaded. I ended up exhausted and still alone. There was no escaping this situation. There was me and only me here. I had to evaluate myself. It was as if all the façade was stripped away. In a moment of sobbing contemplation, I began to realize why some women went back to their bad marriages. On that day, I understood that in certain circumstances even a bad marriage was better than the thought of being alone. And even though it occurred to me that the only man that wanted to talk to me recently was my son, I knew going back to the LCS would never be something I would do.

How did I handle this information? I decided that I needed to listen to the small, still voices that were speaking to me. The word, patience, kept popping up all around me. I went out for Chinese food and my fortune read, "With patience comes happiness." Someone next to me in line at the grocery store was explaining how important patience was to accomplish his job. A character in the book I was reading was named Patience. Everywhere I went I heard the word.

Sitting outside that holiday morning, I wanted so desperately for the phone to ring and for someone to rescue me from my loneliness. I appreciated that I was still learning, and like a chime in my head the word patience kept repeating itself. My heart started to settle down. The tears began to dry up. I had to keep learning this lesson. School was not out yet.

People have many issues that reoccur in their lives. Patience kept rearing its ugly head in mine. As an only child, I tended to have things come to me quicker than to those with siblings. I did not have to fight for the last piece of cake. I did not have to wear clothes that someone else wore. Therefore, when something happened to me the outcome would rectify itself quickly. Living this experience, I knew that a quick resolution was not forthcoming. That acceptance shook something in my core. I felt a temper tantrum making its way to the surface. In the silence of my home, I gave into this. I knew it was immature but I felt unheard and unloved. Self-pity was having a party and I was the only guest, so I threw the mother of all temper tantrums. I cried and uttered the words of all impatient people, "This isn't fair." After I was done, I realized that learning patience was not going to be like a speed-reading course. It was going to hurt, and I would have to suffer. I could not just keep myself so busy that one day I would wake up and patience would have been delivered to my doorstep with a big red bow.

I made a plan for that holiday day. I will be honest and say that it occurred to me to climb back into bed and turn the television on for the rest of the day. I even thought that eating the entire contents of my pantry might help to alleviate the hurt. In the end though, I knew that I had to work through this. I had to find a way to make it through the day. It did not have to be the best day in my life. It also did not have to be the worst. I needed to make it through because I had to make myself understand that deciding to be divorced and to leave my old life meant learning to live with the new life I had. That meant that some days I would have to live with me. Not only that, but I would have to learn to enjoy my own company and know that I was my own best friend. I knew that I could accomplish this task but it was not going to be easy. Let's face it, what had been easy so far? It was another step on the road to healing. I was going to learn that being by myself did not mean that I was unloved or unwanted. Being by myself meant loving me for me, and knowing that I was worth every bit of what I wanted out of life.

I turned on music, because it was hard for me to be depressed when I was listening to Evelyn Champagne King sing "Shame." Then I got dressed and made a plan for myself. If I did what I had planned and made it through the day, then the reward would be for me to feel loved by me. It was a daunting task but one I knew that I could accomplish. Anything else that happened that day would take a backseat to the fact that I was learning to live a new life. I was not going to escape the pain by keeping busy. I was going to walk through the pain and make it to the other side. Once there, I would have progressed. I would have grown. I would have become that much stronger. It would be a hard task to undertake, but I would make it.

After living through this lonely day, I grasped that many other issues in my life needed to be straightened out. I was becoming stronger and stronger every day and I realized that with this strength came certain problems. Not everyone in the world can handle a strong woman. Most people in this world try hard to be strong in one or two aspects in their life. I felt that my strength had been locked in the closet for most of my life and now that it was released, I was going to have to find a way to rein it in. I did not want to become a person that people described as "nice but hard to take." I wanted to be a person that others felt helped and sometimes inspired them.

I knew that helping the women friends in my life was something I was supposed to be doing.

This particular holiday weekend, being alone was little more than self-school. Part of the learning-to-live-with-yourself lesson was incorporated with learning to eat your own words. I spent a lot of time listening to my friends and helping them work out their frustrations and pains. I knew that these same frustrations would show up in me, but I chose not to acknowledge this. On this particular weekend, I not only had to deal with my loneliness but also my expectation and disappointment meter. I had set myself up to believe that certain events were going to take place; and once again that dirty word "expectation" reared its ugly head. Nothing worked out the way I had planned. This compounded the fact that I was alone while my friends had used all my advice and had accomplished their goals. Two of them had found their new loves and were blissfully spending the day cavorting in the soft glow of newfound romance. I was so glad for them! More than anything, I wanted the people who I loved to be happy.

My friend told me, "You are going to have to learn to take your own advice," and this was absolutely true. I was able to encourage others what might aid them in their lives, but I had a hard time listening to the same advice that might help me. I felt that because I had strength, I could surmount all odds by simply bowling the issue at hand right over. Unfortunately, strength had no power over my power of expectation.

I was left without any tools to fight the disappointment that I felt. A friend told me that I created more sadness in my life because I created expectations that were never going to be fulfilled. How right she was. When a woman has created an entire scenario for a weekend, a night, or an event in her head, what creature here on earth could ever live up to the vividness of that imagination?

Along with patience that weekend, I had to learn that I could no longer make expectations. If I did not expect anything, then I would not feel let down when it did not appear. Being strong was never going to make something I expected, happen. I could not bully reality. That weekend I received two lessons for the price of one. Embedded in those lessons was the wisdom that I had earned. I came through the weekend battered and bruised, but I came through the weekend.

CHAPTER FIFTEEN

Coincidence – I think not!

Knowing that I was truly going it alone, I decided that I needed to get help in the dating arena. I mean, let's face it, dating is an art form. Some individuals are artists and others are finger painters. I have lots of paint smeared across my smock, so you can guess what category I fell into. However, I had a friend that while she was a gem in so many ways, she was a glittering diamond because she was a great dater. Let me rephrase that so her husband does not start getting nervous, "She *was* a great dater."

In my twenties, I dated and it was sometimes fun but mostly painful. I never seemed to get the right rhythm. Dating was like dancing. Some people can hear any song and be ready to cha cha with the best of them, and others just step all over everyone's toes. I was a toe-stepper. I always seemed to pick the wrong guy, or the right guy but at the wrong time, or the wrong guy at the wrong time. You get the picture, so in this go-around I knew that I needed help. Flying it solo here was just going to bring a repeat performance of my dating while I was younger, and I did not think my heart or my psyche could take that.

I told my girlfriend about the guy I had been chatting with. I explained the whole situation. Maybe I should explain it to you too. It went like this. A guy contacted me on the wonderful world of on-line dating. He did not have a picture – BIG red flag. However, I was stuck on a cruise with no one to talk to, so I figured I would read his profile. I was intrigued I must say. He was clever and insightful and seemed to be a grown-up. I wrote him when I got home and we started chatting. He (let's call him, George) was witty and sweet and the picture he sent just sealed the deal as he was cute. I soon found out that George was not a closer. More than likely, he had a large range of girls that he was chatting with because he could not make the step to ask any of them out.

We chatted via the internet, and George sent me one of the all-time best emails I had ever received. It belonged in the email Hall of Fame. Of course, me being me, I was already starting to swoon for George and I hadn't even met him yet.

Here is where my dating guru came into play. I laid down the facts to my friend and she told me, "You have only one choice." She told me what to say in the email and to keep it to short sentences. No fluff or small talk was allowed. This criteria was difficult for me but I trusted her. She told me that under no circumstances was I to call, write, email, IM, or send smoke signals to this guy. "Wait." she said.

"Wait?" Did she not realize that I was patience challenged? I followed her rules. I could not believe it. Within one day, George had written me back giving me a night for a meeting. I followed her rules and wrote back with a time and a place, then nothing more. The night of our meeting dawned and I got ready. Now this was not throwing on my cleanest shirt and racing out with my tennies on; this was a dating battle, and for battle I must dress appropriately. I had the perfect balance of sexiness and class. I did not want George to think I would be giving up the goods too easy. I wanted him to know that the goods were there, just high up on the shelf.

My dating guru told me that I must be exactly fifteen minutes late. I was shocked. Late, but that was so rude and disrespectful. I told her that I usually was waiting at the bar when they arrived. She looked at me with arched eyebrows, and I shut my mouth up tight. Okay, I would be late. As it turned out, I was late and not even intentionally. I happened to be caught up in something at home. I rushed out of the house planning to make it only ten minutes late. Yet as I pulled up in front of the restaurant, I realized that my watch was ticking off the last minute of the quarter hour. I got a parking spot right in front, and in I went.

I have to digress a bit here to explain some amazing circumstances surrounding this date. After George had contacted me on-line and we had chatted, I went away with some girlfriends for a wild weekend. During this trip, I was telling the girls about this pen pal when one of my friends said, "What's his name?" I told her, and she started laughing. Yes, she knew him. Not just casually mind you, she had known him for years. They had been divorced at the same time and met at a support group. I know you are thinking, "They slept together." They did not. I got the scoop and then some. I learned the how's and why's to George's divorce. I also learned that he was a serial dater. As my friend put it, "He dates...a lot." I also learned that he was a good guy and wanted a real and true relationship. That was something that I had already surmised from our email pen pal communication. However, there was something good about knowing more than the person I was dealing with knew.

Back to the bar and the first meeting with my potential on-line love. George and I hit it off. We had fun. I was using the force that my dating guru had given me and it was hitting all the right spots just like a light saber. I could almost hear the raspy voice saying, "Use the force…" The date progressed and I knew that things were going well when he kept brushing my leg. The compliments were flying. I was getting dizzy with them. I have to say as a woman who had just endured a marriage without any compliments or attention, I felt like I had just crawled through the desert and someone was dripping water into my mouth.

Now fully entrenched with "the force," I used it to deal the greatest and best blow. When George was describing his good friend that he met when he got divorced, I casually remarked, "Oh is her name…?" The look on his face was priceless. I felt that I had just discovered the new tag for the MasterCard ads. You know the one; new shirt…thirty-two dollars; drink, four dollars; telling the guy you are on a date with, that you know his best friend without his knowledge, priceless. I got that look. George was floored! However, he was also intrigued; and coupled with the incredulity, it worked like a charm.

Hearing my dating guru in my brain, I knew that three hours was the cut-off mark and I had to make my exit. I did it beautifully. He walked me to my car and I hugged him goodbye. By the time I made it home, he had left a message saying that he wanted to see me again.

We did see each other again. Then nothing from me, which further fueled his desire to see me. My goodness, my friend knew her stuff. I had other friends asking if my dating guru friend would be willing to write a how-to book so they could have similar outcomes. At any rate, they wanted to hire her to be a dating consultant. As she was not available to practice this particular calling, my unlucky dating friends had to be happy with my example.

Soon George and I were exchanging wonderful, romantic emails and phone calls. We were head over heels in romance. We saw each other as much as we could and were enjoying each second. It was blissful. It was heavenly. I was falling and it was a freefall.

Before I knew it, we were seeing each other every chance we could. We had even started talking about possibly having a future together. That is when it happened. That is when the eternal other shoe hit. Once again, I was sent spiraling out of dating control. I had made the optimum mistake. I had assumed that this was going to be the one relationship in my life where games would not be taking center stage.

The night that the shoe hit the floor started like any other. I worked and then shopped to make a romantic dinner. Then it happened, and without warning too. Of course, that is not true. There is always warning. After spending a wonderful weekend away together, we returned home and I noticed a shift in the calling and emailing. Not again, I thought. I had already experienced this in Italian, and now it was going to happen in good ol' American slang.

George and I had planned to see each other one night. We both had been busy that day and had not managed to talk personally on the phone. My message light was flashing on my phone telling me that he would be off work at around 6:30 p.m. Expecting that would mean that we would see each other about an hour after that, I waited for the confirmation phone call. None came. Now all the silences and the absence of cute emails were beginning to make sense. This guy was cooling and cooling quickly. Once again, I had misread and misinterpreted the how's and why's of this man's agenda. As the clock rounded the next hour, I started to feel the sinking feeling in my chest. As the next hour ticked away, I could hold it no longer.

As the fates would allow, one of my girlfriends happened to call. She heard the tone in my voice and wanted to know what had happened. I spilled the beans; I also spilled the wine as I attempted to pour my third glass. She told me to stay put because the cavalry was on the way. The friends showed up on my doorstep to a crying and desolate soul. All I could think was once again I was going to be sad and soggy on the couch trying to understand "Why?" I had been out of the game for a while but George had been in hot pursuit, and we both felt the connection that appeared to be growing. It was quickly dawning on me that only one person was connecting. I am sure at this point you are thinking, "When is this girl going to learn?" Good point!

After talking me through the self-flogging that I was giving myself, my friends just listened, then they left. It was two hours and fifteen minutes later, that George called. He was harried and irritated. I asked him to come over so we could talk, knowing that talking about relationships was something most men were not programmed for. I was buoyed by the fact that George was willing to come.

Once he arrived, we talked and his fears and mine spilled out on the same couch we had once been making out on so heavily. He was afraid I was going to go back to the LCS! "Huh?" Where did that idea come from? I was afraid that I was getting too emotionally involved and *he* was not going to be there in the end. It had gone too fast. We did not really know each other. All the stuff was out there now. I felt good about the talking. I did not feel good about the content.

When George left, I had a sinking feeling that this relationship was heading for the door, and all I could do was watch as the lock clicked behind it.

Things started going from bad to worse. Phone calls got less and then more and then less again. After a while, I started to realize that here was another glowing lesson in patience. I had rushed. He had rushed. Now we were at the twenty-yard line with a penalty on the play. Where was this going to go now? I had absolutely no idea. Then another little revelation hit me.

It was not a coincidence that a friend of mine knew George. George and I were both looking for love. All of this happened for a reason. What that reason was still eluded me. I did not have the answers yet. The relationship was still unfolding. I did what any normal woman would do, I let go. I decided that since fate had been stepping in regularly to get us together, it would continue to do so if we were meant to be together. If fate did not want us to be happy in love, then we would not be.

I was done trying to figure out why this was happening. I was done trying to figure out what I had done to create it. It was beyond me. I had to give it up. I had to give it up because otherwise, I was going to make myself crazy wondering what I could do to change the outcome. If George truly was the man of my dreams, then he would continue to be so. If he was not, then the right man was still out there and I needed to be ready when he came.

There was a freedom in letting go. Once I did that I was able to be unconcerned about my actions and statements. The fact of the matter was if I wanted something so bad that I had to make it happen, it might not be the best thing for me. Yet, when I waited and let go for the true outcome to unravel itself, it was invariably the perfect result. All those patience lessons were beginning to rub off. I was ready to cede to fate and let patience stand guard at the door. I was ready to let all the best moments and years of my life that were meant to be, simply be. The tightness in my chest eased, and I started to feel the load be a little less of a burden. I did not want my life to be a burden. I wanted life to be like a wonderful butterfly that flitted its way to me bringing the happiness that I knew I was intended to have. If I allowed for that then there was no way that I could muck it up. It was just saying, "Okay, you know better."

With that, I sat and wrote this chapter. I then turned off the computer, turned off the light, and went to sleep.

What comes between!

I needed more to do. I went to work to ask my partner if she had more hours for me to work. Amazingly, she walked up to me first and asked if I would be willing to work full-time for now. Okay, are you feeling the chills? Just like that, I was working full-time. The work was fun, exciting and all mine. I realized that I was drawing strength from this job. It was more than just the work. It was being with a very dear friend that I had not spent much time with in the last few years. It was exhilarating when I saw that the fates were working in my life. My friend and I had not spent much time together because our lives were in different directions. Yet no matter how long the time between our visits, I always knew that she was there. If I needed her, I could call and she would listen. She had been going through a tough time recently, and it was with this knowledge that I understood that I was supposed to be with her now. I needed her as much as she needed me and by holding each other up, we drew strength. This friend had known my mother. She had loved her too. It seemed like now when there were issues that would some-times weigh me down more than I thought I could take, my friend would say to me, "What would your mother say?" Because she had known my mom, I knew that she could tell me. Interestingly, she often sounded just like my mom. My friend's advice was caring, practical, and forthright. It was she that told me I had to "kiss the mirror" every day. Her advice was not to become vain and superficial, she was telling me I had to love the person I saw staring back at me. Truer words were never spoken. I needed to develop the confidence of my own soul. Where the wealth of strength lived, I needed to plant seeds of self-worth and inner happiness. My friend helped me tend those new attributes as they began to break ground and grow. With her help, I saw my happiness begin to blossom and my self-worth taking root.

I told my friend how obvious it was that she was to help me get through all this muck that I was trekking in. She laughed and said, "I think that you help me through just as much yuck." I grasped how important that dynamic was, as I thought back to all the times my various friends had been there for me. They were always cheering me on, picking me up, and making me laugh just when I needed it. I filed that away knowing that never are we alone on this planet while in this journey through life. This was evident when books came to me with just the right passages that spoke to me. Phone calls that came to rescue me on a night I knew I could not spend one more minute alone. Even the smallest good deed like cookies that appeared on my desk when my PMS was beyond control was proof that my friends were always with me. These angels were at work in my everyday life. With these small and poignant details, it made my life grow to incredible bounds.

Work was a great stabilizer. Little by little, I was drawing confidence into myself and trying to walk a little farther out of the shallow end. One day I found myself making a sales call without realizing I was doing it. When the woman on the other end asked me to send more information, I almost fell out of my chair. My life was progressing and I was moving forward. More than that, I was moving on with great hopes and great goals. I found myself smiling more and crying less. I was standing up straight. I was succeeding.

The first months after the LCS left were very dismal. I remember feeling just dark and small. I knew that this would pass, but when? Now here I was, making sales calls at my new job. I was enjoying nights out in the city with good friends. I was laughing with my children and talking about how we were going to decorate the house for the holidays. I was thinking about the future – my future. I did not think about future as attached to someone else. I was carving a new beginning out of the wreckage of my demolished suburban life.

It was at this time that I went on an official business trip. I had not been on a business trip since before I was married. I was excited but a bit preoccupied because George and I had talked about going together. It seemed that the fates were rubbing my nose in this fact because every seat on the plane was full, except the one next to me. "Ha, ha," I thought. "I get it, I am still alone." I got off the plane at my mid-way point and tried hard not to lose it in the gateway. I called a friend and said, "What do I do? I'm close to having a breakdown in the airport, and I'm afraid that they will come and get me in one of those little cars with the flashing lights." She was smiling on the other end. "Go to the bookstore and buy a fun, light, non-romantic book and then go to the bar and order a drink," she said. I found the perfect book about a husband that tries to kill his wife by throwing her overboard off a cruise ship. She survives and sets to out to destroy her murderous husband in a very cruel manner. It sounded perfect for my mood.

I made it to my destination, New Orleans. As I entered my hotel room I thought, "What do I do now?" I decided to go downstairs to the bar and order myself a drink. I brought my book and sat down at the bar. The bartender and I started talking. I told her how I was supposed to be with someone on this trip. She told me her story about her boyfriend of four years deciding he needed space and was leaving her. We commiserated in the sisterhood of abandonment. She bought me a cosmopolitan, and I ordered dinner. Buoyed by a bit of alcohol and some commiserating, I went to my room and fell asleep.

The day dawned with gray clouds and huge amounts of humidity. I was here in the Big Easy and was interested in seeing as much as possible. I caught a cab down to Jackson Square, oblivious that I could have walked there in ten minutes. I found a seat at the famous Café du Monde and ordered the requisite beniets and coffee. I drank in the atmosphere. The humid and heavy air mixed with the wonderful sax player standing on the corner. The horse drawn carriages were sitting and waiting for the influx of tourists to come. I thought to myself that this was great. It was great to feel so independent.

I went in search of beads to take to the kids. I ended up with way too many chocolate pralines. My cell phone rang, and it was a friend checking up on me. As I stood talking to her, I noticed this man sitting at a table directly across from me. On the table was the sign, "Psychic Readings." I thought to myself that maybe I would go over and talk to him as my phone call ended. Now, everyone who is rolling your eyes - stop! It was amazing. This man took minimal information from me and had me dropping my jaw repeatedly. Mostly it was the fact that here was a total stranger telling me everything about me that most people did not know. I sat with him for an hour as we bonded and he told me that this time was about me. He reiterated a fact I already knew: Everything happens for a reason. I was supposed to be alone in New Orleans. I was supposed to be alone now. Why? To learn, to build, to create a new and improved me. After we talked, I moved straight to a café to write everything down. I was ready to begin the journey that this trip was going to afford me. I was here alone for a reason. Little did I know that the reason was going to be afforded me faster than I could have thought.

I headed back to my room after walking back along the infamous Bourbon Street. It was smaller than I expected. Hearing about it and seeing it on the *Girls Gone Wild* ads made it seem so much wider and longer. It was just a street lined with more bars than I have ever seen in my life. People walked around with alcohol. Other people staggered out of blues clubs. All this occurred at two in the afternoon. I soon learned that New Orleans was a city of excess. Everything that happened, in the week I was there, was that way. Too much alcohol, too much food, too much fun, not enough sleep.

Back in my room, I had a message from another employee of the company. All the people that were staying in this hotel were meeting for a cocktail upstairs at the Concierge Level. I cleaned up and headed upstairs. It was nice to chat about business, since this was a business trip. At the end of the couch was a girl that looked a bit younger than I did. She seemed amused by the whole situation she found herself in. We started talking and were joined by another woman who wanted to go downstairs to the bar and smoke a cigarette and have a "real" drink. Being that this was the land of excess and I could use a drink, I said, "When in New Orleans…" We went to the bar and ordered some real drinks. Over said drinks, I told them my story. The girl from the couch was looking at me and smiling a smile I would see many times that week.

"What?" I asked. She proceeded to tell us that her husband and she had just split up because he had not been a very good boy. She was in the beginning stages of filing for divorce. We were sisters in abandonment from that moment. We did our secret handshake and prepared for a great week.

It was a great week. During the day, we learned lots of information about how to make our business grow. At night, we ended up at the bar in our hotel before that night's adventures. Since we were becoming regulars, we began to know the bar staff. Well actually we met the bar staff the first night we were there. He was cute. He was buffed and strong. He was young and sweet, a very dangerous combination. Here is the best part - he dug me. He was flirting and winking at me. I turned my head around to see if he was looking at someone out the window. Fortified with my requisite vodka, I flirted back. My new friend was giving me the "Go for it," signal. "Please, he is so young, and I am way too old for him." I laughed. As if on cue, he came over and checked on us. "How old are you," my new friend asked boldly.

He was twenty-nine. This adorable, young bartender who was flirting with me was nine years younger than me. Oh, Lord! I was soaring up the stratosphere of self-confidence. I felt Demi Moore was smiling down on me. A twenty-nine-year-old was digging me.

My friend and I continued enjoying the ambiance of the bar. Then we asked our cute bartender where we should go to enjoy the full beauty that was Bourbon Street. He immediately grabbed a pen and started drawing a map for us. He was quick to point out our first stop. The bar offered two drinks for the price of one. That sounded reasonable and practical. This formula of drinking proved to be a lethal combination, but one I would experience often while in New Orleans. After finishing the map that would lead us to intoxication, he asked if he could meet up with us later. My friend said, "OF COURSE!" She told him where we would be, and we set off on our adventure.

Bourbon Street at night was very different from during the day. At night, the smell came out. The smell was indescribable. It was urine, throw-up, sweat, animals, pheromones, and only God knows what else. The first time the scent assaulted my nostrils, I stepped back. I seriously had to think if I wanted to venture further. It was like walking through a curtain of stink. After I stepped forward and committed to the adventure, the smell faded into the background. It was still there, but I did not notice it. I was fixated on the lights, sounds, people, and tumult around me.

We found the first bar and I was excited when I heard the band. They were playing all 80's music. I was home for the night. My friend and I got talked into a drink that sounded good, tasted great, but held disastrous results. Cleanliness is not paramount in New Orleans. The health board does not seem to make many visits to the establishments of Bourbon Street. Therefore, my friend and I were dealt an affliction usually only found in Mexico. We headed back to the hotel and fast.

The next day was work and lots of it. It was great to learn from people who were out there doing the same job I aspired to do, and doing it well. I was motivated to become top producer in a matter of weeks. After a day of expanding our minds, the hosts of our meetings decided they would expand our stomachs as well. Dining in New Orleans was an experience. The excess factor was definitely at play here. No one who was a chef in New Orleans had heard of cholesterol, high blood pressure or clogged arteries. If they have, they do not care. Every item that I consumed was thick with butter, fat, and flavor. Let me tell you that it was heaven. It was so nice not to see the skin picked off the chicken breast. Instead, it was dredged in butter, slapped into more butter, cooked in some butter, and then covered with a fat laden sauce, and it was delicious!

After our food, we adjourned to our bar in the hotel. It had become the meeting place. It did not hurt that my cute, little bartender worked every night. We sat at the bar, flirted, and drank while my friend and I decided where to go that night. Our bartender told us he had gone looking for us last night and had not found us. As he said this, he was looking pointedly at me. I guessed that it might put an end to the flirting if I said that I had protracted Montezuma's revenge at the bar and had to rush back to my room. I told him that we must have just missed him.

He asked if he could meet us tonight. We again agreed. He got my phone number and said he would call us. My friend and I had recruited some other people from our group to join us, and we set off. However, I was wiser now. I realized that I should only drink items that came out of a bottle because then I knew there would not be a repeat of the previous night's demise. The group journeyed through some more '80's tunes. I marveled how most of the people jamming to the songs were not even able to talk when the music had been popular. It was a cruel fact as I realized that my high school years had become retro. It was then that the phone rang. Our bartender was on his way so we were to stay put. We did, he arrived, and we started chatting. Everyone started splitting up and going his or her separate ways as the evening wore on. I determined that it was safe at this point to have the bartender walk me home. It was one in the morning and the lobby of the hotel was devoid of people. The cute, young bartender asked if he could use my restroom. I laughed and said, "Yes." At least he did not ask to see my etchings.

My ego was soaring, as I was kissed and fondled by someone who was nine years younger than I. It was a sweet encounter, and I did not have the guilt or trepidation that I had previously. Everyone needs human contact. I did not spend time trying to undermine the situation. I will not deny that I kept hearing in my head – he is younger than you are and he thinks you are hot. I have to tell you at that moment, the thought of George was deeply pushed into the corner of my mind behind boxes of yearbooks and an old rocking chair. I also learned something else about myself. I was an adult. I was able to be passionate and hungry without huge amounts of emotional baggage being kicked off the bed. It was two consenting adults enjoying a wonderful evening together. Yeah, I know; it was a one-night stand. I'll take it.

I walked a bit taller the next day. I smiled a bit wider too. I was enjoying my life. I was experiencing excess at its finest. Life was good. Hear that? That would be the other shoe. The phone rang and it was George. Here I was trying to make strides forward and the one I had left behind was holding onto my ankle. It surprised me that he was on the phone. It confused me as to why he was calling. How was I supposed to take this? I felt the emotional baggage being stacked back up around me yet again. I felt the box of yearbooks being pushed to the side as George started creeping back into my memory, but this was not the same me. I was not the same person I had been a week ago. Yes, change happens that fast in the new world I lived in. I had received a new agenda with directions, and I intended on following them. Nowhere on the agenda did it say, "Become emotionally attracted again to the man who doesn't know what he wants." So I did not do it. I chatted and said I was having a great time. Behind his words, it sounded as if he was not too happy about that. I knew that going back to George would simply be admitting to myself that I could not progress. That was not a path I wanted to trod upon. I learned from George and our relationship, and that was what I was supposed to do. Now it was time to keep on truckin' down the road to my full and complete self.

The happiest of endings

One night as I washed my face before bed I suddenly realized something. I was waiting for my "happy ending" to finish my story, yet I realized that the life I was living was my ending, and it was happy.

Out of the destruction of a failed marriage, I had picked myself up to become an entirely new person. Let me rephrase that: I had become the person I always wanted to be. I had grieved and mourned my life as a wife. I had grieved and mourned my life as a daughter. I had grieved and mourned my life as a person everyone seemed to leave. My grief had brought me to a place of understanding. Happy endings were not the conclusion of fairy tales; happy endings were where the heroine learned about herself. Happy endings were when the heroine changed. Happy endings were where the heroine survived her turmoil and continued to live.

I took stock of where I was at that point. Standing over the sink, looking at my reflection in the mirror, I realized that I liked what I saw. I saw my eyes looking back at me, and they were wiser. I felt my heart beating in my chest and knew it was stronger. I felt my soul stirring inside and knew it was happier.

I thought about my job. Nine years out of the work force, and a call from a dear old friend brought me to a place where I was challenged and beginning a new career. Even more important, a friendship that had been dormant became alive again. Someone I always had held dear to me became like a sister to me. When I went to work every day, I not only had the excitement of learning something new but I had the joy of being with someone who loved me dearly. I smiled as I drove to work. I laughed every day. My job woke up a part of me that had decided it would be happy just curling up under a blanket for the rest of my life. The job, the connection with the outside world, the rekindling of a love of a friend, it all was the beginning of me as a grown up.

I thought about my children. They were strong, loving, precocious children. They were smart and caring. They laughed, cried, and fought with each other. My children seemed more vibrant and more alive. Perhaps that is because even through their darkest time, they never questioned that they were loved. My children knew that even though the love that their father and I had for each other had died, the love we had for them, never would.

I thought about my friends. I learned very valuable lessons about friendship during this very bleak time. I learned that being a friend to another person is a gift that we are privileged to experience and should never be taken for granted.

Friends are more than just someone to drink coffee with and gossip about the latest scandal. Friends are more than someone to take shopping. They are more than just an ear on the other end of your phone line. My friends were angels put here on earth to help me when I felt that standing up straight was impossible. They were the light in the dark room when I felt that no one would ever love me again. My friends were the hands that held me up when I was not sure whether the weight of this world was much too heavy to bear. Friends are very precious gifts that we unwrap every day in a variety of ways. My friends were the family that I chose. They were the reflection of who I was as a person.

I thought about my strength. How one day a year-and-a-half ago, I could barely get up from the couch, and yesterday I earned an orange belt in karate. I thought about how one day about a year ago, I fell apart when the first man I allowed myself to love after my separation, broke my heart. Yet now I was able to stay home on a Saturday night by myself and feel quite blissful. I thought about how I believed that finding the man of my dreams seemed impossible. Yet after I had healed my fears and insecurities, I knew that one day my dream man would bump into me, trip in front of me, or just catch my eye from across a room and that would be it. I thought about how getting up from that couch and traveling the very bumpy road to healing was the smartest thing I had ever done. I thought about how every day I woke up reading words of encouragement and hope instead of believing words of deprecation and untruth. I thought about how I smiled more than I ever had before, and how I believed in my heart and soul that my life was stronger, happier, and filled with more freedom.

I thought about how God, in his infinite wisdom brought books, tapes, and incredible words into my life to teach me. How I learned that trusting in my choices and myself was an incredible high. I thought about how there are no coincidences in life; and how all the pain, joy, hurt, and love I had experienced in the last year and a half had created in me a belief in kismet, serendipity, karma, and faith. Knowing that those beliefs existed made life so precious to me.

I thought about where I was going. The world was so vast and so attainable. There are no bounds to where I can go and what I can do. I started to believe in dreams again. More importantly, I believed that I could make those dreams come true. I did not need a man to make my dreams alive. I did not need someone else to tell me how to attain those dreams. I could imagine anything and I could achieve anything. I began to think about what I really wanted. I found that even with all the day-to-day sniveling, my list of wants was quite small.

I wanted my children to be happy, healthy, and find the joy in life.

I wanted my life to have meaning by helping others that were in need, especially others that had experienced the same pains I had felt.

I wanted to create. I found the desire to take pictures. I wanted to play the piano more. I wanted to go to an opera. I wanted to smell, taste, and revel in fine cuisine. I wanted to experience all the beauty that the world had to offer.

I wanted to find love. I wanted to wait for the right love. I wanted to know that another heart was searching for mine and one day when the time was right, it would find me.

I wanted to live every day to the fullest. I wanted to laugh loudly and often. I wanted to cry and feel the incredible sweetness of tears rolling down my cheek. I wanted to notice when the sky turned that indescribable color of pink when the sun was either setting or rising. I wanted to glide through the teal water of a tropical sea.

I wanted those I love to find joy and peace in their lives.

I wanted...I realized that my list was longer than I thought. However, no matter how long it was, it was a list of the here, the now, and the future. I did not see the glass half empty any longer. The world was there waiting for me to learn. I had notions to travel to places that I would never have wanted to go to before. I found the yen to try new desires. I realized that in trying something new was where the experience lay.

When this story began, I wanted a fairy tale ending. I wanted the prince to ride up on his white stallion and carry me away. I wanted someone to rescue me from the uncertainty that was my life. I wanted a hero. I wanted a champion. It was a bold and decisive moment in that mirror that I realized – *I* was the champion. I had rescued myself. I did not need a prince because I was already the fairy godmother. I had my happy ending, and the best part of all, was that it was not a happy ending…it was a happy beginning!

Lead a friend to her
Happy Beginning.

Available at
WWW.SCEPTER-PRESS.COM

Fairy Godmother In Training Workshop Series

Lorena Bathey, author of *Happy Beginnings, How I Became My Own Fairy Godmother*, will empower you to take the wand into your own hands. With her encouraging and practical advice – plus a teensy bit of fairy tale magic – you will rescue yourself with your inner fairy godmother and start your own "*Happy Beginning*".

workshop details at
WWW.SCEPTER-PRESS.COM